Why Agree? Why Move?

Linguistic Inquiry Monographs
Samuel Jay Keyser, general editor

A complete list of books published in the Linguistic Inquiry Monographs series appears at the back of this book.

Why Agree? Why Move?

Unifying Agreement-Based and Discourse-Configurational Languages

Shigeru Miyagawa

The MIT Press
Cambridge, Massachusetts
London, England

For information about special quantity discounts, please e-mail special_sales@ mitpress.mit.edu

This book was set in Times New Roman and Syntax on 3B2 by Asco Typesetters, Hong Kong.
Printed and bound in the United States of America.

Library of Congress Cataloging-in-Publication Data

Miyagawa, Shigeru.
Why agree? Why move? : unifying agreement-based and discourse-configurational languages / Shigeru Miyagawa.
    p.   cm. — (Linguistic inquiry monograph)
Includes bibliographical references and index.
ISBN 978-0-262-01361-1 (hardcover : alk. paper) — ISBN 978-0-262-51355-5 (pbk. : alk. paper)
1. Government-binding theory (Linguistics) 2. Grammar, Comparative and general—Agreement. I. Title.
P158.2.M59   2010
415—dc22   2009015564

10 9 8 7 6 5 4 3 2 1

Contents

Series Foreword

We are pleased to present the fifty-fourth in the series *Linguistic Inquiry Monographs*. These monographs present new and original research beyond the scope of the article. We hope they will benefit our field by bringing to it perspectives that will stimulate further research and insight.

Originally published in limited edition, the *Linguistic Inquiry Monographs* are now more widely available. This change is due to the great interest engendered by the series and by the needs of a growing readership. The editors thank the readers for their support and welcome suggestions about future directions for the series.

Samuel Jay Keyser
for the Editorial Board

Preface

One of the great mysteries of human language is the existence of movement operations. Why does movement occur? At every stage in the development of generative grammar, an attempt has been made to answer this
question. It would not be an overstatement to say that the answer at any
given point characterizes in an essential way the general nature of the
theory at that particular point. In other words, every step in the evolu-
tion of generative grammar has been, in no small measure, an attempt
to construct an answer to this question that is better than the one before.
In Government-Binding Theory (GB), movement operations—in fact, all
operations—are entirely optional, so Move α can move anything any-
where, anytime. Independent universal principles such as the Empty Category Principle and Subjacency extract from this overgenerated set of
strings the subset that constitutes the grammatical strings of a particular
language. In this way, the independent principles not only allow the
theory to reach descriptive adequacy—in the ideal, of course—they also
allow it to reach explanatory adequacy in that they "give a general theory
of linguistic structure of which each [grammar of a particular language] is
an exemplification" (Chomsky 1955/1975:77).

In GB, this "general theory of linguistic structure" is the principles-
and-parameters approach, which informs us, among other matters, of
how language acquisition proceeds from the initial state to mastery of a
language. This is a particularly attractive prospect in that we have, in
principle, a clear description of the initial state of Universal Grammar
(UG), and such a description is a principal goal of linguistic theory.
However, there is one problem. These so-called universal principles are
often—perhaps always—a description of the problem. So long as we
depend on such description, we cannot really know the nature of
language—or, more precisely, I-language (Chomsky 1986). This is the
basis for the Minimalist Program (MP), where effort is made to rid the

theory of any element that does not have a natural and independent justification. In an attempt to live up to this ideal, the direction that the theory has taken—although by no means the only direction possible—is to view operations as taking place only as a "last resort" (Chomsky 1993).

Since the early 1990s, at least three classes of movement have been discussed, two of which observe the last-resort nature and a third that does not. One type of last-resort movement is found in the work on linearization initiated by Kayne (1994).[1] On the basis of simple assumptions about hierarchical structure (asymmetric c-command) and its relation to linear order (precedence), Kayne has argued that "[l]anguages all have S-H-C order" (Kayne 1994:47), where *S* stands for *specifier*, *H* for *head*, and *C* for *complement*. This means that SVO (subject-verb-object) is the basic word order, and SOV and other word orders that do not conform to the universal order must have arisen by some obligatory movement. For example, "[i]n an OV language ... the O must necessarily have moved leftward past the V into a higher specifier position" (Kayne 1994:48). Setting aside the precise nature of these movements, the theory predicts that they are obligatory, and further, that they are restricted to cases in which the output adheres to the "antisymmetry" order of S-H.

The second type of last-resort movement is a kind of movement that one might call "EPP-triggered movement" (where *EPP* stands for *Extended Projection Principle*). It is this type of movement that I address in this monograph, taking liberty with the term *EPP* to refer to a broader range of movements than just movement of the subject to Spec,TP. Included in this general type of "last-resort" movement are certain head movements, which I discuss in conjunction with *pro*-drop, and movements of the Ā variety such as *wh*-movement.

The third type of movement is a purely optional movement that has properties very different from the last-resort type. Although it does not adhere to the last-resort nature of the first two kinds of movement, in recent theory it is suggested that optional movement is motivated in that it allows an interpretation that is otherwise not possible (Fox 2000; see also Chomsky 2001, Miyagawa 2005a, 2006). I will not discuss optional movement in this monograph.

Another mystery is the occurrence of agreement systems in natural language. There are two general questions to ask about agreement. First, what is the purpose of agreement? On the surface, agreement appears entirely superfluous in that information in one part of the sentence (e.g., plurality of the subject noun phrase) is repeated in another part of the sentence (e.g., as plural verbal inflection). Moreover, the content of the agreement system sometimes appears patently random, as, for example, in the assigning of gender to noun phrases (e.g., Russian assigns feminine gender to the word *lampa* 'lamp'). Second, why do some languages (e.g., the Indo-European family) have agreement, while others (e.g., languages of East Asia) apparently do not?

The goal of this monograph is to try to answer these questions about movement and agreement. But does it make sense to address, in one work, these two issues that are often handled as distinct phenomena? As it turns out, the answer to one depends on the answer to the other. So it is not only critical that we deal with both—in fact, the two issues at their core must be made to interact with each other in a meaningful way.

Why agree? Why move? The simple answer, I suggest, is that although agreement and movement are the result of distinct operations, they work in tandem to substantially enhance the expressive power of human language. Without agreement and movement, human language would be a shadow of itself for expressing human thought, impoverished to the degree that it would not be able to express such common notions as topic-comment, subject of a clause, focus, and content questions. Crucially, "agreement" here includes grammatical features of topic and focus found in what É. Kiss (1995) has called discourse-configurational languages.

This monograph is organized as follows. In chapter 1, I explore the answer to the question "Why agree?" In chapter 2, I take up the question "Why move?" In the rest of the monograph, I look at the consequences of the analysis presented in the first two chapters. In chapter 3, I suggest a way to unify two types of A-movement, the so-called EPP movement in languages such as English and a class of local scrambling in languages such as Hindi and Japanese. In chapter 4, I examine Kinande and Kilega, both languages of the Bantu family, which exhibit "agreement" and "movement" that are implemented differently but are consistent with the proposed analysis. I also look briefly at Finnish, which shares some elements with Bantu, and I propose a way of distinguishing A- and Ā-movements based on phase architecture. In chapter 5, I explore issues regarding *wh*-questions. I also take up a related issue, the intervention effect invoked by certain elements in *wh*-questions. In chapter 6, I present concluding remarks.

Acknowledgments

This work began in discussions with Noam Chomsky over several years about how to make a minimalist approach relevant to languages that do not have φ-feature agreement—Japanese, for example. I am grateful to Noam for these discussions and for many key suggestions that pushed the project forward at critical junctures. In the fall of 2006, I taught a graduate seminar at MIT with Norvin Richards where I presented earlier versions of the material, and Norvin lectured on material that will appear in *Uttering Trees* in the same *Linguistic Inquiry Monographs* series as this work. Norvin's comments and questions, and those from the students, were enormously helpful in solving some daunting problems and in understanding what needed to be done for this work to see the light of day.

Others in the MIT Department of Linguistics and Philosophy have generously offered their time and advice; these include Sylvain Bromberger, Michel DeGraff, Kai von Fintel, Edward Flemming, Danny Fox, Claire Halpert, Irene Heim, Sabine Iatridou, Michael Kenstowicz, David Pesetsky, and Omer Preminger. I wish also to acknowledge my colleagues Morris Halle and Jay Keyser for their encouragement. I am grateful to many people outside of MIT whose comments I benefited from. There are too many for me to list everyone, but they include Mark Baker, Cedric Boeckx, Vicki Carstens, Gennaro Chierchia, Yoshio Endo, Liliane Haegeman, Nobuko Hasegawa, Anders Holmberg, Jim Huang, Kazuko Inoue, Kyle Johnson, Hisa Kitahara, Jaklin Kornfilt, Jonah Lin, Hiroki Maezawa, Keiko Murasugi, Luigi Rizzi, Mamoru Saito, Miyuki Sawada, Hiroyuki Tanaka, Dylan Tsai, and Yukiko Ueda. Two anonymous reviewers provided extraordinarily detailed and critical comments that helped to shape the final version.

Portions of this work were presented at Harvard University, Kanda University of International Studies, Keio University, MIT, Nagoya University, Nanzan University, National Tsing Hua University, University of

Geneva, and University of Michigan. I thank those who attended these events for numerous suggestions.

I wish to express my appreciation to Pierre Mujombo, the Kinande consultant whom I worked with, for his remarkable insights and for his patience. I thank David Hill for creating the index, Eli Laurençot for assisting with all aspects of preparing the manuscript, and Anne Mark for a terrific job of copyediting the manuscript.

1 Why Agree?

1.1 Introduction

In this chapter, I explore issues related to agreement in human language. Why does agreement occur? Why do some languages appear to have it while others don't? I will begin by demonstrating the direct relation between agreement and movement. I will then make a proposal about the "agreement" and "agreementless" languages that minimizes the difference between them: they are identical in all respects except in what shows up at T or some related head that triggers A-movement. Both typically exhibit movement triggered by a grammatical feature at T; in agreement languages this is ϕ-feature agreement, whereas in agreementless languages it is topic/focus when such a feature occurs, the latter reflecting what É. Kiss (1995) has called discourse configurationality. I will hold in abeyance until chapter 2 a detailed discussion of why movement occurs.

1.2 The Extended Projection Principle

Chomsky (1981) proposed the Extended Projection Principle (EPP) because of the appearance of the expletive in existential constructions (*There stands a statue in the town center*). The agreement is between the verbal inflection and the postverbal nominal, and the expletive *there* fills Spec,TP. The expletive makes it possible for the existential construction with this "long-distance agreement" to have a subject. The EPP is, in fact, informally referred to as the requirement that a clause must have a subject. With the advent of the predicate-internal subject hypothesis (e.g., Kuroda 1988, Sportiche 1988; see also Fukui 1986, Kitagawa 1986), the theory had to account for the movement of the external argument from Spec,vP to Spec,TP, and it is the EPP that has been invoked to drive this operation (Chomsky 1995). To make the EPP applicable to T, Chomsky

(1995) argues that T has a D feature that has to be checked, and attracting a DP (e.g., the external argument) to Spec,TP accomplishes this. Alexiadou and Anagnostopoulou (1998), who argue that this EPP property of T is universal, show that in *pro*-drop languages, rich agreement in the form of a head that contains a D feature raises to T to check this D requirement on T, making it unnecessary for a DP to move to Spec,TP.

Given that the EPP requirement can be met by movement of a DP to Spec,TP (or an agreement element to T) or by merging an expletive on T, one question that this general approach to the EPP raises is this: if there is a choice between movement and merger, is one favored over the other? Chomsky (1995) notes the following pair of examples as evidence that, when either merger or movement is possible to meet the EPP, merger is favored over movement:

(1) a. There seems [TP ____ to be a man in the garden].
    b. *There seems [TP a man to be ____ in the garden].

The lower clause has a T, hence the EPP requirement, and this requirement is filled in different ways in these two sentences. In the grammatical (1a), the expletive *there* is merged on this T to fulfill the EPP requirement, and subsequently moves to the matrix Spec,TP, where it again fulfills the EPP requirement, this time of the matrix T. In the ungrammatical (1b), the EPP requirement of the lower T is met by moving the DP *a man* to its specifier. Under the general approach to the EPP in Chomsky 1995, both options are theoretically available, but the pattern of grammaticality suggests that merger (as in (1a)) is favored over movement if there is a choice between the two, which suggests perhaps that merger is a simpler operation than movement. I will return to this pair later.

A question that arises with the above approach to the EPP concerns the fact that the EPP always appears to operate in tandem with some other element, a point noticed by a number of linguists. If we look at a typical EPP movement, whereby the external argument moves to Spec,TP, we see that two elements are involved besides the EPP: Case and agreement.

(2) [TP He is ____ eating pizza].

The subject, *he*, which has undergone movement to Spec,TP, agrees in Case (nominative) and number (singular) with T. This situation, in which both Case and agreement identify the target of the EPP movement, is typical—in fact, so typical that various linguists have proposed that the EPP should be combined with, or derived from, either Case or agreement. For example, Bošković (1997, 2002) and Martin (1999) argue that an expletive must have Case, and this, according to them, makes it possible to predict its distribution. Behind their studies is the desire to derive the EPP from Case considerations, something they try to accomplish by assuming that Case can only be checked in the specifier position of the head responsible for valuing Case (e.g., T) (Boeckx 2000, Epstein and Seely 1999; see also Koopman 2003, Koopman and Sportiche 1991). In contrast, Chomsky (2000, 2005, 2007, 2008), Kuroda (1988), Pesetsky and Torrego (2001), and I (Miyagawa 2005b), among many others, suggest that the EPP is identified with agreement.

Which is the right answer for the EPP—Case or agreement? Or is the EPP simply an independent phenomenon, as previously and still widely assumed (e.g., see discussion in Landau 2007)? Looking only at languages such as English, which is the language in which the EPP has been most extensively studied, it is difficult to tease apart the different components to get at the exact identity of the EPP. To find compelling evidence, we have to go beyond the familiar languages whose EPP properties have been investigated.

A number of languages display a phenomenon called "agreement asymmetry" in which the agreement on the verb differs depending on whether the subject occurs pre- or postverbally.[1] In the Northern Italian dialects of Trentino (T) and Fiorentino (F), verbs do not agree with postverbal subjects; the verb instead has the unmarked neutral form (third person masculine singular) (Brandi and Cordin 1989:121–122).

(3) a. Gli è venuto delle   ragazze.   (F)
    b. E'   vegnú qualche putela.   (T)
      is   come   some   girls
      'Some girls have come.'

Full agreement on the verb—agreement in number, in this case—is not allowed with postverbal subjects, as shown in (4).

(4) a. *Le son   venute   delle   ragazze.   (F)
    b. *L'è   vegnuda qualche putela.   (T)
      they are come   some   girls
      'Some girls have come.'

In contrast, full agreement must occur, as in (5a–b), if the subject moves to preverbal position (presumably Spec,TP) (Brandi and Cordin 1989:113).[2]

(5) a. La Maria la   parla.   (F)
    b. La Maria la   parla.   (T)
      the Maria she speaks
      'Maria speaks.'

Presumably, the subject is Case-marked in both pre- and postverbal positions. Consequently, the pattern of grammaticality found in these Northern Italian dialects clearly shows that the occurrence of agreement correlates with movement. If agreement occurs, the subject must move to Spec,TP; but if there is no movement, agreement does not occur.

In certain agreement asymmetries, the asymmetry is between partial and full agreement. A well-known asymmetry of this type is found in Arabic: a postverbal subject triggers partial agreement of person and gender as in (6a) (the verb also has the default singular agreement form), whereas a preverbal subject triggers full agreement of person, gender, and number as in (6b) (e.g., Bahloul and Harbert 1993, Benmamoun 1992, Fassi Fehri 1993). The following examples are taken from Bahloul and Harbert 1993:15.

(6) a. Qadim-a (/*qadim-uu) al-ʔawlaadu.
    came-3MS   came-MP   the-boys-3MP
    'The boys came.'
  b. Al-ʔawlaadu qadim-uu (/*qadim-a) [*t*].
    the-boys-3MP came-3MP   came-3MS
    'The boys came.'

What we can deduce from these Arabic data is that, just as we saw with the two Northern Italian dialects, agreement triggers movement. Unlike in the Northern Italian dialects, where no agreement emerges if movement does not take place, in Arabic, person and gender agreement appears when there is no movement. Number agreement cannot occur if there is no movement, but number agreement, along with person and gender agreement, must occur if the subject moves to preverbal position. This clearly shows that number agreement is responsible for movement. Arabic demonstrates that, although it is correct to associate agreement with movement, not all agreement forms are equal in this regard. In this monograph, I abstract away from these interesting but complex issues regarding various types of agreement and focus by and large on the general point that agreement, not Case, triggers movement.

Returning to the pair in (1) from Chomsky 1995, repeated here, we can see that the "agreement" approach to the EPP provides an alternative account of these examples.

(7) a. There seems [TP ____ to be a man in the garden].
   b. *There seems [TP a man to be ____ in the garden].

Given that the lower TP is nonfinite, it has no agreement; hence, there is no reason for anything to move to the specifier of this lower T. That is why (7a) is grammatical; Spec,TP is not filled (the gap should in fact follow *to* to show that there is no "EPP" within this TP). In contrast, in (7b) *a man* has moved to this specifier—an instance of unmotivated movement, hence ungrammatical. On this account, we need not specify that merger takes precedence over movement, a desirable outcome given the recent assumptions about these two operations. Bošković (1997, 2002) offers an alternative to this pair based on Case considerations. If we limit our data only to English, it is difficult to choose between the two approaches, but the data from agreement asymmetries in Arabic and Northern Italian indicate that agreement is the correct option.[3]

One of the achievements of the Minimalist Program (MP) has been to unify merger and movement under the general operation Merge, where external Merge covers what used to be the domain of phrase structure and X-bar theory, and internal Merge takes over what used to be the domain of movement (Chomsky 2000, 2001, 2005, 2007, 2008). Both are exactly the same operation, the only difference being what is merged. External Merge takes an item from the numeration, so that what is being merged is being merged for the first time. Internal Merge takes something that is already in the structure and remerges it. An important result of unifying the two operations is that the theory is able to account for a key insight from the Standard Theory era by Emonds (1976). Emonds observed that movement operations lead to structures that are identical to those produced by phrase structure rules, a phenomenon he called "structure preservation." Given the pre-MP theory, there was no reason why structures that result from movement should be identical to those built by phrase structure rules. On the other hand, Merge, external or internal, predicts the structure-preserving nature of movement: movement is simply another instance of Merge. Ideally, then, we want to avoid making any qualitative distinction between the two types of Merge, such as a preference for one over the other when both are possible. We can accomplish this by adopting the agreement approach to the EPP. (Case would work, too, but recall the data from agreement asymmetries.) Of course, we have more to do to make this work; but both conceptually and empirically, there is ample justification for pursuing this line of reasoning. I now turn to the question of why agreement occurs in human language.[4]

1.3 Why Agree?

What is the purpose of agreement? Many linguists have asked this question, from a variety of perspectives, but nothing close to a consensus has emerged. What is particularly striking about agreement is that, on the face of it, it seems to be entirely superfluous. In its most basic form, the "agreement rule," let us say, targets information in one position—the information contained in a nominal such as the subject—and reproduces it in another position, commonly as some form of an inflectional element on a verb or some such "head." In (8a), the verb inflects for singular, whereas in (8b), the lack of overt inflection indicates plurality—in both cases reflecting the nature, singular or plural, of the subject.

(8) a. Mary walk*s*.
    b. They walk.

This redundant nature of agreement is puzzling. Why should human language contain a rule that represents information redundantly? There are other domains of language where information is repeated—for instance, pronominalization—but the repetition is informative.

(9) John thinks that he will win the race.

John and *he* are repetitive, to the extent that they refer to the same entity in discourse, but they do not reproduce the same information: *John* is the subject of *think* and *he* is the subject of *win*, so these two occurrences provide distinct information.

The puzzling nature of agreement goes further. In the Russian example in (10) taken from Corbett 2006:2, not only is the singularity of the subject redundantly reproduced on the verbal inflection, but its grammatical gender is as well, and the choice of feminine gender for a lamp is patently arbitrary—there being nothing inherent about lamps that would make them feminine.

(10) Lamp-a   stoja-l-a   vugl-u.
     lamp(F)-SG stand-PST-F.SG in.corner-SG.LOC
     'The lamp was standing in the corner.'

So, agreement is not only redundant, but sometimes entirely arbitrary in its content as well.

Given these puzzling properties, what could the purpose of agreement possibly be? Levin (2001) points to a variety of functional approaches that appear in the literature, most of which boil down to the idea that the redundancy helps the addressee accurately comprehend the information by repeating it across the expression. Such a proposal faces the difficulty of accounting for the wide variety of agreement systems that exist in languages, including, most critically, lack of agreement, as in the East Asian languages. Are East Asian languages simply nonredundant in communicating information relative to, say, subject-verb?

Although there is no consensus on the outer boundaries of what constitutes agreement, there is reasonable concurrence that agreement is a form of *covariance* between two elements, such as the covariance between the subject nominal and verbal inflection (Steele 1978:610). Various studies assume this notion of covariance for agreement (e.g., "feature sharing" in Pesetsky and Torrego 2007). Furthermore, many of these studies describe covariance as an asymmetric relation, whereby one element, the goal/controller, in some fashion is deemed the source of the information for the probe/target (e.g., Anderson 1992, Chomsky 1965, 2001, Gazdar et al. 1985, Keenan 1974, Pesetsky and Torrego 2007). There are other approaches, such as the unification-based frameworks (Pollard and Sag 1994, Shieber 1986), that reject the asymmetric, "copying" approach, instead positing that agreement emerges from an accumulation of information from a variety of sources in the structure. I do not pursue the unification approach in this monograph.

I am now ready to begin to answer the question, what precisely is the purpose of agreement? Up to now we have seen that the formal agreement system is redundant in that it comprises a covariance of two or more elements, each expressing the same information. It is asymmetric, in that one of the elements participating in the covariance relation provides the agreement information. Finally, the semantic content of the agreement information is apparently not significant, and may even be arbitrary, as in the case of the feminine gender on 'lamp' in Russian. We find all three properties represented in the probe-goal system of Chomsky's work (Chomsky 2000, 2001, 2005, 2007, 2008). A *probe* (the "target" of agreement) is an *uninterpretable feature* by virtue of not having a full value for its feature; for example, it is unvalued for gender. The *goal* (the "controller" of the agreement) provides the value, thereby accounting for the covariance and the asymmetric nature of agreement. Finally, an uninterpretable feature must be deleted once it is valued so that it will not receive semantic interpretation, a fact that directly reflects the notion that the actual content of agreement is irrelevant. Although the probe-goal system captures the essential properties of formal agreement, it makes the notion of agreement all the more puzzling. Why would the computational system insert something into the derivation of an expression only to delete it so completely that nothing remains of it for semantic interpretation? It seems utterly counterintuitive.

The answer to the true identity of agreement, I suggest, is based on what is sometimes referred to as "the duality of semantics": the well-established distinction between lexical and functional heads. Lexical heads select their complements to create the argument structure of an expression. In contrast, functional heads, which are commonly merged higher than the basic argument structure, create an expression structure that "consists of the modes of expression of the language" (Bresnan 2001:9–10). The functional layer of a clause gives rise to such notions as topic-comment, subject of a clause, focus, and content questions, among many other modes of expression. In other words, *functional heads substantially enhance the expressiveness of human language.*[5]

I will call the relations found in the argument structure *lexical relations*, for the obvious reason that these relations are defined over a lexical head and its argument, typically a head-complement relation. The nominal— and the complement is almost always a nominal, although in certain cases it is a PP or a CP—bears a particular relation to the lexical head such that its referent is understood to be a participant in the event or the situation described by the meaning of the head. I will call the second type *functional relations*, since they always involve a relation between a nominal and a functional head, such as C, T, or v. As noted above, the purpose of functional relations is to enhance the expressive power of language by providing the tools to express such notions as topic-comment, subject of a clause, focus, and content questions.

We can see the independence of functional relations from lexical relations in a number of constructions. For example, in Japanese, the reflexive anaphor *zibun* 'self' is subject oriented. In the following example, *zibun* can only take as its antecedent the subject *Taroo*:

(11) $Taroo_i$-ga $Hanako_j$-o $zibun_{i/*j}$-no-heya-de sikat-ta.
     Taro-NOM Hanako-ACC self-GEN-room-in   scold-PAST
     'Taro scolded Hanako in his/*her room.'

However, under direct passivization, the internal argument, *Hanako*, may function as the antecedent of *zibun* (Kuno 1973), which shows that the notion "subject" plays a crucial role independent of lexical relations.

(12) $Hanako_j$-ga $Taroo_i$-ni $zibun_{*i/j}$-no-heya-de sikar-are-ta.
     Hanako-NOM Taro-by self-GEN-room-in   scold-PASS-PAST
     'Hanako was scolded by Taro in her/*his room.'

The original external argument, *Taroo*, no longer the subject of the overall expression, cannot function as the antecedent of *zibun*.

How are the two types of relations, lexical and functional, established in the linguistic structure? Lexical relations are thematic relations. They are established by external Merge, in which a lexical head (or v) combines with its complement in a binary fashion (Chomsky 2001, 2005, 2008, Kayne 1984). Lexical relations are therefore defined by the binary-branching structure of sisterhood, itself created by external Merge. What about functional relations? There is no simple structural way to establish a relationship between, say, the external argument and T. T does not directly select the external argument, for example. (I discuss the expletive construction, which is ostensibly a counterexample, in chapter 2.) In the literature on this topic, a typical suggestion is that the relation that holds between a functional head such as T and the nominal with which it agrees (or assigns Case to) must be established by moving the nominal into Spec,TP (Koopman 2003, 2005, Koopman and Sportiche 1991). In the main, I believe that this intuition that agreement emerges as a specifier-head (Spec-head) relation is correct, although there are exceptions, one being *pro*-drop. Nevertheless, I will assume that agreement relations are established independently of movement, by a process Chomsky calls *Agree* (Chomsky 2000, 2001, 2005, 2008). We can thus state the purpose of agreement as follows:

(13) *Purpose of agreement*
Agreement occurs to establish a functional relation.

I will capture the Koopman-Sportiche intuition that agreement requires a Spec-head relation by showing that Agree takes place to establish functional relations. Such a functional relation, which is always nonlocal, must be transformed into a local relation by moving the goal to the probe. The purpose of this movement is to keep a record of the functional relation beyond narrow syntax so that semantic interpretation and information structure can make use of it. This, in effect, is Spec-head agreement, but implemented as two independently motivated operations—Agree and Move.[6]

Pesetsky and Torrego (2006) and Sigurðsson (2004, 2006) independently argue that Agree, or some form of probe-goal relation, exists for all instances of Merge, external and internal. These proposals in one way or another blur the distinction between lexical and functional relations. It is quite possible that something must trigger even external Merge, as these studies suggest. However, I will distinguish between functional and lexical heads, as noted earlier, and presume that the kind of Agree relation I wish to explore here is relevant only to functional heads. After all, we never see formal agreement inflection reflecting a relation between a lexical head and its argument; such inflection is found only between a functional head and some XP. This is the Agree relation I wish to capture.[7]

There is another proposal, very different in nature, that also blurs the distinction between lexical and functional relations. Chomsky (2007) suggests that the edge feature is responsible for Merge, both external and internal. Note that the edge feature is independent of Agree. The edge feature brings us back to something akin to GB in one respect: in principle, it allows free movement—free internal Merge—to any head. The grammar simply has to ensure that the movement is motivated. Although I will not include the edge feature in the narrow syntax, I assume with others that movement must be justified, and that where agreement is concerned, the justification is that movement brings the goal close to the probe. In chapter 2, I discuss the notion of closeness in detail and what precisely it accomplishes.

As a final note on why agreement occurs in human language, the picture I drew above provides a natural way to think about which categories count as phases (Chomsky 2001). In recent minimalist work, it is thought that computation in language, such as the numeration and Merge, occurs within specific local domains called *phases*. Once the computational system completes its work within one phase, the products of this computation are sent to PF and semantic interpretation, and the computation then goes on with its work in the next higher phase. What are these phase categories? Chomsky (2001, 2005, 2007, 2008) proposes that minimally they are CP and vP. From the perspective taken here, these two categories comprise the two principal parallel structures in language: the *expression structure* and the *argument structure*. CP is the complete expression structure, and vP is the complete argument structure. Chomsky (2001) uses the notion of completeness as well; in the approach taken here, phases have a highly specific and concrete underpinning—that is, the phases comprise the two principal structures that the computational system builds to create the expressions of a language.

I have given an explanation for why agreement occurs in human language. I now turn to the second question about agreement: why does it occur in some languages but not in others?

1.4 Agreement, Topic/Focus, and Strong Uniformity

1.4.1 Strong Uniformity
We saw that in subject-verb agreement languages such as English, a subject moves to Spec,TP if there is agreement inflection on T that agrees with it. Otherwise, there is no reason for the subject to move, and it stays in the position where it was externally merged. It was Kuroda (1988) who

proposed that movement is forced under agreement. Further, he proposed that agreementless languages such as Japanese do not force movement; instead, any movement that might be observed occurs as an entirely optional operation (see Saito 1989, 1992 for the view of scrambling as a purely optional operation). I agree with Kuroda that agreement, as opposed to Case, triggers "forced" movement. But does an agreementless language such as Japanese involve no forced movement at all? I will argue that in discourse-configurational languages, of which Japanese is one, something else that is computationally equivalent to ϕ-feature agreement triggers forced movement.

I will argue that in discourse-configurational languages, topic/focus establishes functional relations in the same way as ϕ-feature agreement in agreement languages. I hasten to add that it is not the case, for example, that agreement languages do not also have focus, or that discourse-configurational languages do not have ϕ-features. In fact, we will see that all languages have both kinds of grammatical features: ϕ-features and topic/focus features. Much of the monograph will address how particular languages deal with this uniform set of features. Work by Cinque (1999) and the cartography linguistics of Rizzi (1997, 2004) and others hint at this idea that all languages have essentially the same universal features/structures.

The overall approach that I adopt here rests on the *Uniformity Principle* (Chomsky 2001:2).

(14) *Uniformity Principle*
In the absence of compelling evidence to the contrary, assume languages to be uniform, with variety restricted to easily detectable properties of utterances.

My approach is very much in line with that of Sigurðsson (2003), who assumes this Uniformity Principle literally for all languages and suggests the Silence Principle, by which he means that any given language shares the universal set of features with all other languages but does not pronounce all of them. This is, at least in part, the reason for the differences among languages. Here, I will adopt an even stronger interpretation of the Uniformity Principle and assume that, at least for grammatical features such as agreement and focus, every language not only shares a uniform set of features but also (contra Sigurðsson) overtly manifests these features in some fashion. Although this assertion is part of the Uniformity Principle—in fact, if I am right, it is a strong affirmation of this principle—I will give it a name for ease of exposition and call it *Strong Uniformity*.

(15) *Strong Uniformity*

All languages share the same set of grammatical features, and every language overtly manifests these features.

For example, Japanese, which shows no agreement inflection except in rare cases such as subject honorification, nonetheless is predicted to have φ-feature agreement in some form, as I will attempt to show. In chapter 2, I will show that Chinese, another "agreementless" language, in fact evidences person agreement.

This strong interpretation of the Uniformity Principle cannot be right for all features of a language. After all, languages do vary. In adopting the strong version at least for grammatical features, I intend to explore some of the outer bounds of the Uniformity Principle.

1.4.2 Discourse-Configurational Languages

It has long been observed that in many languages a phrase identified as topic or focus undergoes movement. Such a language is what É. Kiss (1995) describes as *discourse-configurational*.

(16) *Discourse-configurational languages*

a. "In a topic-prominent language, the topic is, in a way, an alternative to the subject [in a subject-prominent language] as the VP-external argument." (É. Kiss 1995:4)

b. "Focus movement is triggered in some languages but not in others." (É. Kiss 1995:5)

É. Kiss notes that in many discourse-configurational languages, both topic and focus are associated with movement, although there are languages where only one is. In a paper very much related to discourse configurationality, Grewendorf (2005) has argued that the movements in the German middle field that have typically been characterized as scrambling are nothing but topic or focus movement. Although I differ from Grewendorf in not assuming specific projections that host topic and focus, I will demonstrate that in Japanese both topic and focus trigger movement just as in German, and that the movement is equivalent to the movement caused by φ-feature agreement—A-movement to Spec,TP or some related "A" position. In this way, in discourse-configurational languages, topic/focus has the same role as φ-feature agreement: both establish a functional relation. Here, I will briefly describe the discourse-configurational nature of Japanese, holding a more extensive discussion in abeyance until chapter 3.

In Japanese, there are cases where movement is forced, but what forces it is not φ-feature agreement. Rather, these movements are triggered by topic or focus. The term *topic* as I am using it refers to the entity the sentence is about. It is close to, but different from, *discourse topic* in that, for example, a topic need not refer to an anchored expression in the conversation; it simply needs to be characterizable as "what the sentence is about." A sentence with a topic falls into the class of expressions that Kuroda (1972–1973) calls "categorical" as opposed to "thetic," a distinction he bases on the logical theory of Marty (1918, 1965). Japanese has a topic construction where the topic, marked by *wa*, is always the discourse topic (Kuno 1973). The topic construction that I will discuss is different: here, something is moved and is given the property of topic in the broad sense of "topic of the sentence." I will argue that topic/focus in Japanese constitutes a grammatical feature that is computationally equivalent to φ-feature agreement in forcing movement that results in A-chains. The idea that focus in some languages functions as a grammatical feature that drives movement has been suggested by a number of linguists (see, e.g., Brody 1990, Horvath 1981, 1986, 1995, É. Kiss 1995). Below, I will give one example of focus in Japanese that results in A-movement; in chapter 3, I will give evidence that these focus movements in Japanese undergo A- and not Ā-movement.

In Japanese, a *wh*-phrase can be interpreted as an indeterminate pronoun in the context of the universal quantificational particle *mo*. This combination of *wh-mo* is a negative polarity item.

(17) Taroo-ga *nani-mo* kawa-nakat-ta.
 Taro-NOM what-MO buy-NEG-PAST
 'Taro didn't buy anything.'

As is well known, the *wh*-phrase portion and *mo* can be separated (Kuroda 1965, Nishigauchi 1990).

(18) Taroo-ga *nani*-o kai-*mo* si-nakat-ta.
 Taro-NOM what-ACC buy-MO do-NEG-PAST
 'Taro didn't buy anything.'

Here, the *wh*-phrase as an indeterminate pronoun occurs in object position with the accusative case marker -*o*, and the universal quantificational particle *mo* occurs on the verb stem. One distinct property of the indeterminate pronoun expression is that it is typically associated with focus— meaning something like 'absolutely nothing/no one'. I will assume that the indeterminate pronoun is associated with the focus feature, which is licensed by *mo*; it is this focus feature that gives the indeterminate pronoun this "identificational focus" interpretation (but see note 8).

I will make use of Kishimoto's (2001) analysis of the indeterminate pronoun. As noted above, the indeterminate pronoun is a *wh*-phrase that is interpreted as an indeterminate pronoun in the context of the universal particle *mo*. Kishimoto proposes that in order for the *wh*-phrase to be interpreted as an indeterminate pronoun, it must be dominated by the same immediate maximum projection that dominates *mo*; that is, *mo* and the indeterminate pronoun must occupy the same minimal domain. As part of his analysis, Kishimoto argues that the verb raises to v in Japanese, taking *mo* with it, as shown in (19).

(19)

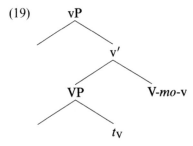

In this structure, *mo* can license any indeterminate pronoun in its local vP. In Kishimoto's analysis, the object is assumed to move to Spec,vP. This is why it is fine to have an object indeterminate pronoun like the one in (18). As a piece of evidence for his analysis, Kishimoto observes that an indeterminate pronoun cannot occur in subject position.

(20) **Dare-ga   piza-o   tabe-*mo* si-nakat-ta.
      who-NOM pizza-ACC eat-MO   do-NEG-PAST
      'Anyone didn't eat pizza.'

Kishimoto assumes the EPP here and argues that the subject indeterminate pronoun *dare* 'who' raises to Spec,TP to satisfy the EPP requirement of T; this movement takes it outside the scope of *mo*, which is on v. This, then, is a case of forced movement that takes a phrase to Spec,TP. Instead of ϕ-feature agreement, what is operative here is focus.[8]

There is further evidence for this analysis beyond Kishimoto's data. First, recall from (18), repeated here, that the indeterminate pronoun is fine in object position.

(21) Taroo-ga *nani-o*   kai-*mo* si-nakat-ta.
      Taro-NOM what-ACC buy-MO do-NEG-PAST
      'Taro didn't buy anything.'

Now observe what happens if we scramble the object to the head of the sentence.

(22) *Nani-o$_i$ Taroo-ga t_i kai-*mo* si-nakat-ta.
     what-ACC Taro-NOM   buy-MO do-NEG-PAST
     'Taro didn't buy anything.'

As shown, if the object indeterminate pronoun is scrambled to the left of the subject, the sentence becomes ungrammatical. What does this fact indicate? Kishimoto's analysis does not predict this ungrammaticality. The problem is that this kind of scrambling may be A-movement, which is what we are attempting to analyze, but it may also be Ā-scrambling. Ā-scrambling allows reconstruction (Mahajan 1990, Saito 1992, Tada 1993), so that in (22), the moved object indeterminate pronoun *nani* should in principle be interpretable in its original complement position. This should lead to a grammatical sentence. We can see the Ā-movement possibility of local scrambling in (23), where an anaphor has been moved to the head of the sentence.

(23) Zibun-zisin-o$_i$ Taroo-ga t_i hihansi-ta.
     self-ACC   Taro-NOM   criticize-PAST
     'Self, Taro criticized.'

The fact that the indeterminate pronoun in (22) cannot be so reconstructed indicates that it has undergone A-movement, which normally does not reconstruct. In Miyagawa 2001, 2003 (see also Hasegawa 2005, Kitahara 2002), I argued that the landing site of this kind of A-movement is Spec,TP. This is what we predict if focus in discourse-configurational languages like Japanese functions as a grammatical feature that triggers A-movement. In chapter 3, I will give evidence for the "A" nature of this movement. There, I will also revise the view that the movement always takes place to Spec,TP; I will suggest instead that it can sometimes move to an A-position above the TP, which I will call αP.

Let us return now to the agreement–topic/focus parameter. An immediate problem arises with the idea of such a parameter. Take focus, for example. Focus and agreement are usually thought to be located on fundamentally different heads. Focus is commonly postulated to occur on the focus head that is higher than T and in the region of C (e.g., Culicover and Rochemont 1983, Rizzi 1997), or, in languages such as Hungarian and Turkish, possibly lower (see É. Kiss 1995 for discussion of various approaches). In contrast, agreement in (for example) subject-verb agreement is normally construed as being located on T. Although it is not entirely implausible for two features on fundamentally different heads to vary parametrically, the idea of an agreement–topic/focus parameter would be more plausible if focus and agreement were not found on such vastly different heads. There is sufficient evidence to associate focus with a head higher than T, so if we are to do anything about "head parity," we need to look at agreement. To get right to the point, I suggest, following Chomsky (2007, 2008), that agreement in (for example) subject-verb agreement is associated with a head higher than T—namely, with C (see Boeckx 2003, Carstens 2003, Kornfilt 2000, 2004 for a similar idea). There are conceptual and empirical reasons for assuming this. Conceptually, merging the agreement feature on C means that grammatical features that are responsible for computations such as movement show up solely on phase heads—C, v, and possibly D, although I will limit my discussion largely to C. Given that any operation beyond initial Merge takes place within phases, it makes sense that the elements triggering these operations are merged on phase heads, ϕ-feature agreement being one such element.

There is also empirical evidence for assuming agreement to merge on C. First, in English, environments where agreement (and Case) is not assigned, such as the ECM (exceptional-Case-marking) construction, involve a "bare" TP that does not have a CP (Chomsky 2005, 2008). A simple way to view this is that C provides the agreement, and in its absence, T by itself cannot bear agreement (or Case). A second piece of empirical evidence is that agreement actually shows up on C in some languages. For example, Carstens (2003:393) notes the following West Flemish examples (from Haegeman 1992):

(24) a. Kpeinzen *dan-k* (ik) morgen   goan.
        I.think   that-I (I) tomorrow go
        'I think that I'll go tomorrow.'
     b. Kpeinzen *da-j*   (gie) morgen   goat.
        I.think   that-you (you) tomorrow go
        'I think that you'll go tomorrow.'
     c. Kvinden *dan*   die boeken te diere   zyn.
        I.find   that.PL the books too expensive are
        'I find those books too expensive.'

Although a number of linguists have proposed that the complementizer-subject agreement is an instance of the agreement on T raising to C (Hoekstra and Marácz 1989, Watanabe 2000, Zwart 1993, 1997), Carstens argues that the agreement originates on C (see Carstens 2003 for additional references for and against this idea). One piece of evidence is that the complementizer must be adjacent to the subject it agrees with. In (24a–c), the embedded verb also inflects for agreement, which suggests that the agreement also shows up on T. Under my analysis, which closely follows Chomsky's (2007, 2008) proposal, this suggests that the agreement on C may percolate down from C to T, a point I discuss later.

The picture that emerges is that both topic/focus and agreement initially occur on C, as shown in (25). (I use the generic term *ϕ-probe* for the uninterpretable ϕ-feature agreement at C.)

(25) *Uniform set of features*

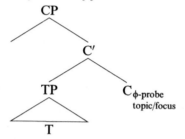

Technically, what is merged on C is an uninterpretable feature. For agreement, it is an uninterpretable agreement feature, the ϕ-probe, that must be valued by the interpretable feature on the goal (Chomsky 2000, Pesetsky and Torrego 2006). For focus, what is the nature of the uninterpretable feature? Expanding on a line of investigation in Holmberg and Nikanne 2002, I propose that there is just one feature for topic/focus, and it is the "default" topic feature, −focus. If this feature enters into agreement with a focused element, it is turned into a +focus feature. Details will be given in chapters 3 and 4.

The topic/focus feature is matched with a relevant phrase in the structure—for example, the thematic subject. In most cases, this category is raised to Spec,TP because that is the head the probe ultimately ends up on by inheritance from C. One ostensible exception is long-distance agreement, where the goal appears to occur lower than the head with the ϕ-probe. I will take up the issue of long-distance agreement in chapter 2 and show that for many cases, long-distance agreement in fact is not an exception to the need for agreement to form a Spec-head relation. Another exception to the idea that the ϕ-probe and its goal occur in the Spec,TP region comes from Bantu: we will see instances where the ϕ-probe occurs on a projection higher than TP, which I call *αP*, the same projection I will posit for some of the topic/focus movements in Japanese (for detailed discussion, see chapter 3).

By initially placing agreement as well as topic/focus on a "high" head in the C region, we make it plausible for these two features to be the two polarities of the same parameter. Because agreement and topic/focus constitute the primary grammatical features in the proposed system, we also thereby isolate all such features on a phase head, C. This is a desirable outcome: agreement and topic/focus are two major elements of computation in narrow syntax, and the idea of isolating them initially on C means simply that we identify the major elements of computation with phase heads—C, v, and possibly D. Although I will not have much to say about v and D, I will explore this view in detail with regard to C. Indeed, if topic/focus and agreement are essentially two sides of the same coin as far as computation is concerned, we gain a conceptual argument that agreement should be associated with C. There is sufficient evidence that topic/focus is associated with the C domain (see, e.g., Culicover and Rochemont 1983 for focus). If agreement has the same formal function as topic/focus—to trigger movement—then it would be conceptually plausible to locate agreement at C as well.

But do topic/focus and agreement constitute a natural class independent of syntactic movement? If so, there is a plausibility argument to add to our empirical and theoretical arguments. Historical analysis suggests a relation between topic/focus and agreement. It is widely assumed that subject agreement morphology historically develops from subject pronouns (e.g., Givón 1976). Givón proposes that the process by which this happens relates to topicalization. When something is topicalized, it typically leaves a pronoun in its original position. The idea is that this pronoun in the topic construction gets reanalyzed and becomes part of the verbal morphology. Alternatively, Simpson and Wu (2001) suggest that the subject pronoun's reanalysis as agreement morphology has to do with its being associated with focus. On either account, there is a clear link historically between agreement and topic/focus, which lends further credence to my claim that these features are computationally equivalent.

A major point I will illustrate is that in a discourse-configurational language, topic/focus, which occurs on C, ultimately shows up on a lower node such as T, triggering A-movement to this lower node. In certain cases, the head that ultimately hosts topic/focus may be a head higher than T and lower than C, as I demonstrate in chapter 3, but for the time being I will keep the picture simple and assume that in these languages topic/focus appears on T. This means that the topic/focus feature that starts out on C is inherited by T, as shown in (26).

(26) *The topic/focus feature is inherited by T in a discourse-configurational language*

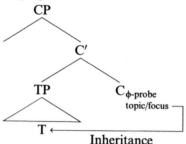

This agreement–topic/focus parameter boils down to whether the topic/focus feature is inherited by T. If it is, the structure will represent a discourse-configurational language as described by É. Kiss (1995, etc.) and others. I will discuss this inheritance of topic/focus by T in detail in chapters 3 and 4.

What about the φ-probe? In earlier work (Miyagawa 2005b), I assumed that the φ-probe also has the option of staying on C or being inherited by T. This assumption was based on an analysis of Kinande as described by Baker (2003). However, in chapter 4, I will present an alternative analysis of the Kinande facts that shows the φ-probe being inherited by a lower head other than T. What this means is that the φ-probe, if it occurs, is apparently always inherited by a lower head regardless of whether the topic/focus feature is also inherited (see Chomsky 2007, 2008), as shown in (27).

(27) *The φ-probe is always inherited by a lower head such as T*

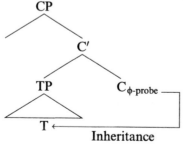

What is the reason for this inheritance? There are two questions here: why inheritance occurs at all, and why φ-probes are always inherited by a lower head. Concerning the first, I will assume the reason Chomsky gave when he originally proposed feature inheritance (Chomsky 2005, 2008): it enables languages to have A-chains. Without inheritance by T, all movement would be Ā-movement; that is, all movement would be operator movement. Language would be deprived of movement for purposes of informational structure, such as creating subject-of relations, topic-comment relations, and so forth. From the perspective of the agreement–topic/focus parameter, this means that in some languages, such as English, A-chains are created on the basis of ϕ-probe inheritance, but in the discourse-configurational languages, they are created on the basis of topic/focus.[9] A central question of this monograph is, then, what happens in constructions in a discourse-configurational language where both the ϕ-probe and topic/focus appear? I take up this question particularly in chapter 4 when I look at Kinande and Kilega (both Bantu languages) and at Finnish.

Let us turn to the second question: why ϕ-probes are always inherited by a lower head. If the ϕ-probe is always inherited in this way, an objection that one might raise to the overall approach outlined so far is, why not simply merge the ϕ-probe at T to begin with? That was, in fact, the assumption prior to the recent works by Chomsky and others. We have seen conceptual and empirical arguments that favor merging the ϕ-probe at C. When we look at Bantu and Finnish, we will see cases where the ϕ-probe is not inherited by T; rather, it is inherited by a head higher than T but lower than C, which I call αP.

(28)

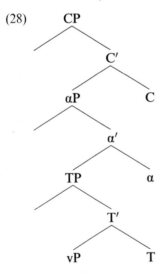

This type of projection between TP and CP, illustrated in (28), has been proposed for a variety of languages, including Bantu (Baker 2003), Hungarian (É. Kiss 1995), and Romance (Uriagereka 1995). Particularly in

the case of Bantu, the φ-probe at α gives rise to interactions between the
φ-probe and movement that differ sharply from the familiar Indo-
European situation where the φ-probe typically picks out the grammatical subject and it is this subject that moves to Spec,TP. Being inherited
by a higher head, the φ-probe in Bantu is able to pick out any DP in its
search domain, so that what raises may be the subject, the object, or the
locative (the locative in the Bantu languages we will look at is apparently
a DP), and the raised phrase—the subject, the object, or the locative—is
what enters into agreement with the φ-probe. (The following examples
are from Baker 2003:113.)

(29) a. Omukali mo-a-seny-ire   olukwi (lw'-omo-mbasa). (SVO)
          woman.1 AFF-1.S/T-chop-EXT wood.11 LK11-LOC.18-axe.9
          'The woman chopped wood (with an axe).'
     b. Olukwi si-lu-li-seny-a   bakali (omo-mbasa). (OVS)
          wood.11 NEG-11.S-PRES-chop-FV women.2 LOC.18-axe.9
          'Women do not chop wood (with an axe).'
     c. ?Omo-mulongo mw-a-hik-a   omukali.   (LocVS)
          LOC.18-village.3 18.S-T-arrive-FV woman
          'At the village arrived a woman.'

In (29a), the verb agrees with the subject 'woman'; in (29b), it agrees with
the raised object 'wood'; and in (29c), it agrees with the raised locative 'at
the village'. We have to assume that for the object or the locative to be in
the local search domain of the φ-probe, it must occur at the edge of the
vP (Carstens 2003). In chapter 4, I will draw on Baker's (2003) work to
show that the agreed-with phrase (subject, object, or locative) occurs
higher than Spec,TP.[10]

Why is the φ-probe that occurs at α in Bantu free to pick out any DP in
its search domain, while a φ-probe at T is limited to the grammatical subject? One possibility is that in "subject agreement" languages such as English, there is no reason for a DP within vP—typically the object—to
move to Spec,vP, so that such a DP can never find itself in the local domain of the φ-probe in the higher phase. On this account, the fact that the
φ-probe at T only picks out the grammatical subject is coincidental in the
sense that it is only the grammatical subject that appears in its search domain. We can discount this approach by looking again at Bantu. We will
see that in certain constructions, the αP is disallowed, so that the φ-probe
is forced to be inherited by T. When this happens, a very different pattern
emerges, exactly like the pattern in the familiar Indo-European languages: the φ-probe must pick out the grammatical subject. Since we

know that the Bantu languages allow the object or the locative to enter into the search domain of the φ-probe at α, it cannot be the case that when the φ-probe occurs at T, the object and the locative are blocked from moving to Spec,vP to be visible to the φ-probe.

A more promising idea is to view φ-probes as incapable of identifying a goal by themselves. A goal must somehow be "activated" to be visible to a φ-probe, and the mechanism that typically activates it is Case (Chomsky 2001). Let us assume the traditional view (somewhat different from the view in Chomsky 2001) that T assigns nominative Case; in minimalist parlance, T values the Case on its target, which is the grammatical subject (e.g., Pesetsky and Torrego 2001). The φ-feature at T then picks out the target of this Case assignment—the nominative subject—as its goal. This is why the φ-probe at T always picks out the grammatical subject.[11] What about the Bantu case? The φ-probe is inherited not by T but by the higher head α, which is not a Case assigner. In chapter 4, I show how this φ-probe on α together with the topic feature, which is also inherited by α, accounts for the several possible goals the probe can seek— subject, object, or locative. As I also show, this analysis can explain Baker's (2003) polysynthesis parameter without stipulating that Case does not play any role in Bantu.

The reason, then, that the φ-probe is inherited by a lower head is that it must seek a way to find its goal, being unable to do so by itself. The situation is different for focus, for example. Focus is usually marked in discourse-configurational languages—in Japanese, for example, it is morphologically marked, as we will see in chapter 3 and especially in chapter 5. There is no need to activate the goal, and therefore the probe is able to pick out its goal without depending on some activation mechanism. What about topic? We will see in chapter 3 that topic is fundamentally different from focus and also from the φ-probe in that it does not seek a goal in the sense of a probe-goal relation. It is similar to focus, though, in that the probe responsible for topicalization does not require activation of the goal.

Although I will not take up Case in this monograph, it does play an important role particularly in tandem with the φ-probe. Case's role in activation is prominently discussed in recent minimalist literature (e.g., Chomsky 2000, 2001). I assume that it has other roles to play as well, one of which is to make a nominal phrase visible for θ-marking, an assumption from GB (Chomsky 1981). This is perhaps its main role. After all, while we find inherent Case, which is Case that comes with a particular θ-role, we never find inherent agreement. The so-called default agreement in antiagreement is a lack of agreement, not some inherent agreement. On this view, Case is primarily an entity in the domain of *lexical relations*, although it is typically assigned by a functional head such as T, whereas agreement is an entity in the domain of *functional relations*. Where the two come together is in those situations where a φ-probe, in establishing a functional relation, takes advantage of the ability of Case to make a nominal visible for θ-marking.

The above discussion makes clear when Agree takes place for the φ-probe and focus (regarding topic, see chapter 3). Whereas both the φ-probe and focus begin at C, the φ-probe does not enter into an Agree relation until it is inherited by a lower head that has an activation mechanism, most commonly Case. At this point, Agree takes place and a goal for the φ-probe is identified. In contrast, the focus feature requires no activation, so it enters into an Agree relation when it is at C. Notice that this raises an issue for complementizer agreement in West Flemish. How can the φ-probe at C be valued? I return to this problem in chapter 2.

The strong version of the Uniformity Principle that guides this work predicts that a language like Japanese, which is considered to lack φ-feature agreement, should manifest it in some fashion. Let us look next at this prediction.

1.4.3 Evidence for Person Agreement in Japanese

The strong interpretation of the Uniformity Principle assumes that all languages share the same essential components. This means that all languages share the features we are looking at, φ-features and topic/focus, which are both merged initially on a phase head. Recall that Strong Uniformity does not state that these two features must always be present. Rather, every language has both, and we should be able to find them in some given construction in every language.

Although Japanese does not show the typical subject-verb agreement found in many languages, it does exhibit person agreement involving elements that occur higher than T, in what Inoue (2006) calls D(iscourse)-modals. These modals, which arguably occur in the C domain, express some sort of attitude on the part of the speaker toward the utterance and also typically the hearer. Many traditional Japanese grammarians have examined issues of modality in the language and have found that these modalities often impose a limitation on the kind of subject that is allowed—person agreement, in other words. Examples (30)–(34) are from Ueda (2006:168–169, 174), who based them on examples in Nitta 1991; see also Tenny 2006 for relevant discussion.

(30) *Exhortative [first person, *second person, *third person]*
{Watasi/*Anata/*Yamada-sensei}-ga Taroo-ni tegami-o
I/*you/*Prof. Yamada-NOM   Taro-DAT letter-ACC
okuri-MASYOO.
send-let's
'Let's (have) me/*you/*Prof. Yamada send Taro a letter.'

(31) oku *[first person, *second person, *third person]*
{Watasi/*Anata/*Yamada-sensei}-wa Taroo-ni tegami-o okutte
I/*you/*Prof. Yamada-TOP   Taro-DAT letter-ACC send
OKU.
OKU
'I/*You/*Prof. Yamada will send a letter to Taro.'

(32) *Prohibition [*first person, second person, *third person]*
{*Watasi/Anata/*Yamada-sensei}-wa Taroo-ni tegami-o
*I/you/*Prof. Yamada-TOP   Taro-DAT letter-ACC
okuru-NA.
send-don't
'Don't *I/you/*Prof. Yamada send Taro a letter.'

(33) *Negative supposition [first person, *second person, third person]*
{Boku/*Kimi/Kare}-wa iku-MAI.
I/*you/he-TOP   go-probably.not
'I/*You/He probably won't go.'

(34) *Assertion (see also Inoue 2006) [first person, *second person, third person]*
{Watasi/*Anata/Yamada-sensei}-wa Taroo-ni tegami-o
I/*you/Prof. Yamada-TOP   Taro-DAT letter-ACC
okut-TA.
send-PAST.ASSERT
'Asserted: I/*You/Prof. Yamada sent a letter to Taro.'

Exhortative (see (30)) and *oku* (see (31)) only allow the first person; prohibition (see (32)) only allows the second person; negative supposition (see (33)) and assertion (see (34)) only allow first and third persons. There may be other such modalities. For example, Ueda (2006:174) lists questions as only allowing second and third person, but that may simply be a matter of the meaning—normally, a speaker does not ask about an action or event whose subject is the speaker himself or herself, though in the right context, it should be possible.

Another example of φ-feature agreement in a discourse-configurational language is provided by the so-called force markers in Korean (examples from Pak 2006:295–296).

(35) a. *Imperative*
Cemsim-ul mek-e-*la*!
lunch-ACC eat-IMP
'Eat lunch!'
b. *Exhortative*
Icey kongpwuha-*ca*.
now study-EXH
'Now, let's study.'
c. *Promissive*
Nayil   nay-ka cemsim-ul sa-*ma*.
tomorrow I-NOM lunch-ACC buy-PRM
'I will buy lunch tomorrow.'

Although earlier studies of these force markers treat them as distinct construction types, Pak notes that the markers share several syntactic traits: in embedding, none allows an overt subject; they do not allow mood particles; they allow a special negative marker, -*mal*; there is no tense marking; and they can be conjoined by -*ko*, which requires conjuncts to be the same type of clause. The following examples demonstrate the force markers' ability to occur with -*mal*.

(36) a. *Imperative*
Mek-ci **mal**-a-*la*.
eat-NOM NEG-A-IMP
'Do not eat.'
b. *Exhortative*
Mek-ci **mal**-*ca*.
eat-NOM NEG-EXH
'Let's not eat.'
c. *Promissive*
Mek-ci **mal**-u-*ma*.
eat-NOM NEG-U-PRM
'I promise not to eat.'

Pak concludes that these particles all represent the same type of construction and, specifically, that they all involve agreement at C.

There are two further points to be made about these particles. First, as Pak notes, the restrictions found in person with these markers are imposed on the subject, and they appear best specified as ±speaker, ±addressee. This makes sense because at the C level, which is the interface with the universe of discourse, the two participants are the speaker and the addressee. Pak proposes the following characterizations:

(37) a. Imperative: −speaker, +addressee
   b. Exhortative: +speaker, +addressee
   c. Promissive: +speaker, −addressee

The imperative marker -*la* indicates that the subject is the addressee, the exhortative -*ca* indicates that the subject is the speaker and the addressee together (expressed using the first person inclusive of the addressee), and the promissive -*ma* indicates that the subject is the speaker. The same approach applies by and large to the person restrictions observed earlier for Japanese.

The second point has to do with how valuation of the φ-probe proceeds. All of the Japanese and Korean examples of person agreement at C involve some element, typically associated with modality, such as the exhortative -*masyoo* and negative supposition -*mai* in Japanese and the force markers in Korean. It is the presence of one of these elements that imposes the person agreement/restriction. Crucially, it is not the subject that values the φ-probe at C, as is commonly the case in agreement languages. Later I will speculate on why the subject does not value the φ-probe in Japanese, but right now let us work through how valuation takes place. First, it is important to note that the kind of person restriction found in Japanese does not always occur; it emerges only when one of the relevant modal elements appears in the construction. If there is no such modal, there is no person restriction; hence, there is no φ-feature agreement. This is still consistent with the Strong Uniformity interpretation of the Uniformity Principle: it simply shows that in Japanese, φ-feature agreement does occur, but not in every clause.

When the φ-probe does occur, I suggest that it is inherited by the modal head, as shown in (38), and the modal head, which contains the interpretable person feature, values it at that point. This suggestion is based on the intuition that it is the modal that imposes the person agreement.

(38)

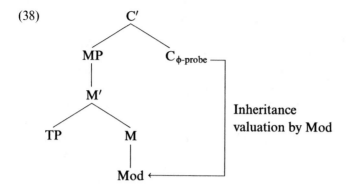

I am supposing here that the φ-feature, by attaching directly to its goal, is able to undergo valuation because it does not have to seek the goal through some activation mechanism. Now the φ-feature has a value; let us say it has been valued as first person by the goal Mod. The valued φ-feature is now almost like a clitic in that it has an agreement value, and it needs to be able to impose this restriction. But given that it is a φ-probe, it cannot assert its value by itself; instead, it has to depend on some other mechanism. Case is the natural candidate, so the φ-probe is inherited by T, where the person restriction on the subject is imposed through the nominative Case assigned by T. This is shown in (39).

(39)

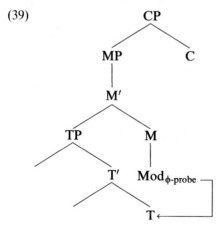

One final question regarding person agreement in Japanese and Korean is, why does it work the way it does? Unlike the typical φ-feature agreement, where a φ-probe seeks its goal inside TP, in Japanese and Korean a modal is the goal that values the φ-probe. I speculate that this is because nominals in Japanese and Korean are not associated with the appropriate interpretable person features to value a φ-probe. The only other possibility is Case, and the nominal phrase that is picked out is the "subject," similarly to what happens in languages like English. Why does the Japanese and Korean nominal lack φ-features? One possible answer could come from Chierchia's (1998) nominal parameter. Chierchia argues that nominals are parameterized for whether they can refer to individuals (e.g., English) or just to kinds (e.g., Japanese). We might speculate that nominals that can only refer to kinds do not have the appropriate content for carrying interpretable φ-features. We will see in chapter 2 that Chinese, the language that Chierchia uses to demonstrate the "kind" type of nominal system, turns out to have a robust person agreement similar to the ones found in Indo-European. But this will not negate the idea that the "kind" nominal cannot carry φ-feature agreement. As we will see, the actual goal of the φ-probe in Chinese is an empty agreement head, similar to those studied by Alexiadou and Anagnostopoulou (1998) in Greek. Even in Chinese, the fully specified nominal does not appear capable of valuing the φ-probe. I will leave this issue open.

1.5 Summary

In this chapter, I posed two questions about agreement: why does agreement occur, and why do some languages have it while others do not? I suggested that agreement establishes what I call a functional relation between a functional head and an XP. Unlike lexical relations, which are strictly local, any relation between a functional head and an XP must be established by some rule that can relate two points, often two distant points, in the structure. Agreement is tapped for this purpose in languages that have φ-feature agreement. The relations that are established between functional heads and XPs are critical: they substantially enhance the expressive power of human language by making it possible to express such notions as topic-comment, subject of a clause, focus, and content questions.

To explain why agreement occurs in some languages but not others, I first proposed that all languages have a uniform set of features that includes φ-features and topic/focus and that all languages should display overt evidence of both. I called this proposal Strong Uniformity, reflecting the idea that it is a stronger version of Chomsky's (2001) Uniformity Principle. In some cases, such as person agreement in Japanese and Korean, φ-feature agreement does not occur in every sentence; instead, it arises in constructions involving a variety of modals. Moreover, I argued that topic/focus in discourse-configurational languages such as Japanese has a function equivalent to φ-feature agreement in agreement languages in triggering A-movement. So, the difference between agreement languages and discourse-configurational languages boils down to what triggers movement at T: the φ-probe or topic/focus. I suggested that topic/focus and φ-feature agreement are both merged on a phase head (C being the primary phase head that I dealt with) and that the φ-probe, if it occurs, is inherited by T or some related head.

The difference between agreement and discourse-configurational languages boils down to whether or not the topic/focus feature is also inherited by a lower head such as T. If it is inherited, we have a discourse-configurational language, but if not, we have an agreement language. Of course, agreement also occurs in discourse-configurational languages, and, as we will see, how it functions differs from one discourse-configurational language to the next. This issue of variability among discourse-configurational languages will be a focus of the discussion in chapters 2–4.

2 Why Move?

2.1 Introduction

Chapter 1 dealt with the question, why does human language have agreement? My answer was that agreement, or its discourse-configurational counterpart, topic/focus, establishes functional relations—that is, relations between a functional head and an XP. Functional relations occur at a distance because the functional head must "reach down" into the argument structure layer of language. Agreement and topic/focus, which connect two points in the syntactic structure, are designed specifically to create these links that occur at a distance. The ultimate purpose of agreement (and topic/focus) is to imbue language with expressive power that it could not otherwise have.

In this chapter, we turn to the second big question—why does human language have movement? I will limit the discussion to movement operations that are (1) closely tied to agreement of some sort and (2) forced (i.e., obligatory). I will exclude movements characterized as optional; for this type of movement, see Fox 2000 and Miyagawa 2005a, 2006, among others.

2.2 Movement Is a Record of Functional Relations

In chapter 1, we saw that the presence of an agreeing element, which includes ϕ-features and topic/focus, leads to movement. Specifically, the goal of the agreement moves to the specifier of the head that has the uninterpretable agreeing feature—what I have called the ϕ-probe. For ϕ-feature agreement, the uninterpretable nature of the probe means that this ϕ-probe is a feature that has not been fully specified. For example, an uninterpretable feature for number may simply be αnumber, and α must ultimately be valued as singular or plural in languages with singular/plural number agreement, such as English. In recent theory (e.g., Chomsky 2001, 2005, 2007, 2008), this valuation takes place when the uninterpretable feature finds its goal (the controller of the agreement), which contains a fully specified, hence interpretable, version of the feature—for example, singular. This is the operation Agree (Chomsky 2001). We saw in chapter 1 that the Agree relation for the φ-probe is established after the φ-probe is inherited by T. Under Agree, which links the probe with the goal, the goal values the uninterpretable feature of the probe, so that αnumber takes the value singular. We might come up with a more refined formalism, but the point is clear. For topic/focus, I will lay out a similar system of valuation in chapter 3.

According to Chomsky (2001, 2005, 2007, 2008), valuation occurs under Agree, so that as soon as the probe enters into an Agree relation with its goal, valuation ensues. Under a different view (Bobaljik 2006, Pesetsky and Torrego 2006, Sigurðsson 2004, 2006), Agree is kept separate from the process of valuation; Agree is a purely syntactic process by which two positions in the syntactic structure are identified as being in a relation. A proposal that extends separation of Agree and valuation is to view valuation as taking place in the morphological component, a part of PF (for the proposal that morphology is part of PF, see Halle and Marantz 1993). This is essentially the position taken by Bobaljik (2006) and Sigurðsson (2004, 2006), who suggest that agreement is a matter of morphology.

I will stay with the idea that Agree and valuation are part of the same operation, where Agree establishes the probe-goal relation, and the goal then values the probe. This is the simplest assumption to make, and it enables us to address the central concern at hand—namely, the nature of movement. This way of looking at Agree parallels, for example, θ-marking, the only difference being that θ-marking is always strictly local, so there is no need for an operation like Agree to identify the target of the θ-marking operation. It is important to point out that, whereas valuation takes place in narrow syntax as part of Agree, the actual phonological features for the agreement values presumably are assigned in the morphological component, which is assumed to be part of PF (Halle and Marantz 1993). There is at least one possible exception to the idea that valuation takes place in narrow syntax. Later in this chapter, when we return briefly to the West Flemish data on complementizer agreement, I will speculate that the complementizer portion of the agreement receives its valuation not in narrow syntax but in PF. But this is an isolated case; the more typical instances of valuation take place in narrow syntax as part of Agree. We will see that, despite this difference in valuation, the complementizer agreement data provide evidence that φ-probes begin at C.

Recall the way that agreement is invoked by the probe-goal pair. The φ-probe is an uninterpretable feature that must be valued by the interpretable feature on the goal. Recall, too, that the purpose of agreement is independent of the content of agreement—it is to establish a functional relation. Now let us consider what happens to the φ-probe in the derivation. Before it reaches semantic interpretation, it must be erased (Chomsky 2001, 2005, 2007, 2008). The reason is simple. It makes no sense for semantics to interpret a φ-probe on a head, even if it is valued by the goal. To give one example, it makes no sense for semantics to interpret +feminine on T. Deleting the φ-probe scrubs the string clean of material superfluous to semantic interpretation. But now we have a problem. The probe-goal relation is established to create a functional relation between a functional head and an XP, but if the φ-probe is erased before the string is transferred to semantic interpretation, there will be no record of the functional relation that has been created. Semantic and information-structure interpretation will never "know" that a functional relation was ever established between a functional head and an XP. Functional relations are established across a distance, to bridge the functional layer and the argument structure layer, and if the φ-probe is erased, this link will be lost. This is where movement comes in. By moving the goal to the probe, human language has figured out a way to keep a record of functional relations for semantic and information-structure interpretation, in the absence of φ-probes. This, I believe, is the true reason for movement, although the way it is actually implemented by the probe-goal mechanism does not readily reveal this reason.

(1) *Why move?*

Movement triggered by agreement takes place in order to keep a record of functional relations for semantic and information-structure interpretation. Given the architecture of human language, movement is the *only way* to preserve functional relations beyond the interface to interpretation of semantics and information structure.

In other words, language ensures that functional relations, which significantly enhance expressive power, become part of the semantic and information-structure interpretation of the sentence by forcing movement. Of course, within narrow syntax, operations of agreement and movement take place as formal computation, and they are not motivated by considerations of meaning, expressiveness, and related matters. But the effect they have is to make the output of narrow syntax effectively usable as an entity imbued with enormous expressiveness. In the next section, I provide the technical details of what it means for the goal to move to the probe, but the intuition is clear: movement takes place to retain a record of the functional relations created initially by the operation of Agree. The diagram in (2) illustrates what I have just described (see also Chomsky 2007).

(2)   Narrow syntax: The goal is moved to the probe

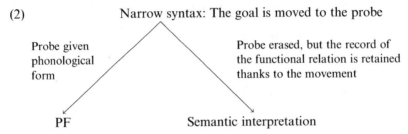

Probe given phonological form

Probe erased, but the record of the functional relation is retained thanks to the movement

PF   Semantic interpretation

The probe can survive in PF, where it is given phonological form (in most cases). It does not receive semantic interpretation because it has been erased, but by this time it has done its work of establishing a functional relation and forcing movement to retain a record of that relation. In this way, we can account for the intuition developed in earlier studies (e.g., Koopman 2000, 2003 and earlier works) that agreement always involves a Spec-head relation. In discussing movement, I use the term *specifier* in the traditional sense, although in the current system (bare phrase structure; see below) there is no "specifier" per se. I use the term strictly for expository purposes, just as I use traces (*t*) and bar levels (X, X′, XP), other carryovers from earlier practice.

2.3 How Movement Retains a Record of Functional Relations

To see how movement retains a record of functional relations, I turn to the concepts in the bare phrase structure approach to structure building (Chomsky 1995:241–249). In earlier work, a phrase such as *the book* is characterized as having the structure in (3).

(3)

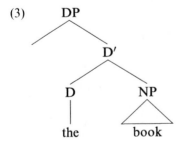

In the bare phrase structure approach, bar levels are dispensed with (see Muysken 1982), and only the minimal and maximal nodes (D and DP above) are visible at the interface (Chomsky 1995:242). Furthermore, the label for the maximal projection is defined to be identical to its head. The phrase *the book* would therefore have the informal characterization in (4), informal because an item such as *the* is technically a bundle of features.

(4)   the

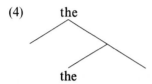

the

Merge builds structures by pairing two items, $\{\alpha, \beta\}$, one of which projects to give the new item its label, either α or β.

Suppose that a ϕ-probe α, an uninterpretable feature, occurs on a head, X, which has the goal β. The diagram in (5) illustrates the structure prior to the movement of the goal β.

(5)   X

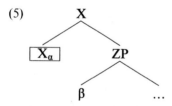

The head X projects as the label for the constituent that contains X and ZP. The label is the same as the head. Therefore, when the goal β moves to the "specifier" of X, it merges with the label of the head that contains the probe.

(6)

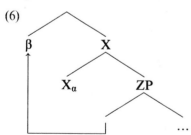

This movement has the effect of transforming the nonlocal relation established by Agree into a strictly local relation created by Merge, as stated in (7).

(7) *Probe-goal union (PGU)*
    A goal moves in order to unite with a probe.

With this local structure in place, even when the φ-probe is erased prior to semantic interpretation, the functional relation established between X and β is unmistakably retained for use in interpretation.

In effect, the goal moves to the specifier of the head that contains the probe. This explains the intuition that agreement requires a Spec-head relation (e.g., Koopman 2000, 2003). The idea isn't that agreement must be represented in a Spec-head relation; rather, the Spec-head relation makes it possible to attain PGU, which in turn retains for semantic interpretation (and other relevant interpretations such as information structure) the functional relation that was established by Agree, which itself does not require a Spec-head relation in order to apply. An obvious problem with this view is the expletive construction, which appears to license agreement without any movement. I will turn to this construction in the next section and show that an analysis in the literature on expletives makes this construction consistent with the PGU proposal.

Two other questions arise concerning movement as I have described it. First, if, under the bare phrase structure approach, both the head and the label are the same, are there cases where the goal raises directly to the head instead of to the label to implement PGU? The answer is yes; these are the cases of *pro*-drop in which a pronominal head containing rich agreement raises to T and values the probe at T, making it unnecessary to raise an XP to the specifier of TP (see Alexiadou and Anagnostopoulou 1998). I will comment on this in more detail below.

Second, at what point in the derivation does PGU take place? Clearly, it must take place before transfer to semantic interpretation.

(8) PGU must be established by the point of transfer.

I have been assuming the existence of phases, a phase being a complete unit of argument structure (vP) or expression (CP) (Chomsky 2001). In Chomsky 2001, it is not the entire phase that is transferred (or "spelled out"); rather, it is only the interior (or "complement") of the phase. This gives rise to the Phase Impenetrability Condition. For example, once a CP is built, what is transferred is its complement, TP. Because the edge of each phase remains intact for the next phase, elements are able to pass from one phase to the next, as in the case of long-distance *wh*-movement.[1]

What ultimately is pronounced in the specifier position of the head that contains the probe may be the goal that fulfills the PGU requirement, as in the case of the external subject in Spec,TP, or it may be a copy of the goal. A copy in Spec,TP, for example, is fully capable of establishing

PGU so long as it is a fully specified copy. In chapter 4, we will look at when a moved element leaves such a copy, but for the time being I will assume that, whereas Ā-movement arguably leaves a full copy, A-movement need not do so, although it can. Thus, the tail of an Ā-movement is always able to fulfill the PGU requirement. In the rest of this chapter, I will draw on studies in the literature to demonstrate PGU and the fact that it must take place at the point of transfer.

Finally, the basic tenet of this monograph—that topic/focus plays a role in discourse-configurational languages that is computationally equivalent to the role of ϕ-features—suggests that topic/focus in these languages should undergo the kind of valuation found with ϕ-probes in agreement-based languages. This is different from the standard view of topic/focus; for example, for focus it is typically assumed that there is a focus head that carries the interpretable focus feature (e.g., Brody 1990; in chapter 3 I discuss this matter extensively). In chapters 3 and 4, I will develop a probe-goal system for focus in the discourse-configurational language Japanese. I will suggest that topic works somewhat differently, although it is in line with the overall assumptions of my theory.

2.4 Expletives and Related Matters

I now turn to expletives, which, on the surface, appear to be an exception to the PGU requirement.

Expletives have played a major role in the development of a number of important aspects of GB and particularly in the Minimalist Program. Chomsky (1981) based the Extended Projection Principle (EPP) on the appearance of the expletive in examples like (9).

(9) There entered a boy into the room.

In more recent frameworks, the appearance of the expletive in such examples made it possible for T to enter into so-called long-distance agreement with the postverbal nominal phrase (here, *a boy*), which led Chomsky (2000, 2001) to decouple agreement from movement. In this construction, then, the agreement does not require movement; instead, it may exist as long-distance agreement, where the goal is not in the specifier of the head that contains the probe. Under this view, expletives would be an exception to PGU. Below, I will present an alternative account that is consistent with the view that agreement requires PGU to obtain. Later in the chapter, I will take up other well-known cases cited as evidence for long-distance agreement in languages such as Hindi-Urdu and Itelmen, and show that they too have an analysis compatible with PGU (although problems remain).

A number of linguists have made proposals about the nature of expletives. Bošković (1997, 2002) and Martin (1999) argue that an expletive must have Case and that this makes it possible to predict the distribution of expletives. Behind their studies is the desire to derive the EPP from Case considerations, something they try to do by assuming that Case can only be checked in the specifier position of the head that is responsible for valuing Case (e.g., T) (Boeckx 2000, Epstein and Seely 1999; see also Koopman 2000, 2003; Koopman and Sportiche 1991).

Another approach looks at expletives as the realization of the D feature (Chomsky 1995:364; see also Lasnik 1997). Given that D is the locus of ϕ-feature agreement, this would mean that an expletive carries the feature(s) that function as the goal of the probe under Agree. The "EPP" effect would follow naturally from this relationship, given that the goal must raise to the probe to value it. What would be involved is not Case, as the linguists mentioned above suggest, but ϕ-feature agreement associated with D—a state of affairs that would make the appearance of an expletive equivalent to the appearance of a DP.

What precisely is the source of expletives? A number of linguists have argued that an expletive begins in the vicinity of the associate noun phrase (e.g., Chomsky 1995). For Moro (1997), an expletive is a predicate, and for Sabel (2000) it occupies D in the structure that contains the associate noun phrase (see also Choe 2006, Kayne 2006 for relevant discussion). The following examples, with some additional detail, are from Sabel 2000:414:[2]

(10) a. [$_{TP}$ *There* [$_{T'}$ is [$_{DP}$ *t* a man] in the garden]].
    b. [$_{TP}$ *A man* [$_{T'}$ is *t* in the garden]].

In (10a), the expletive *there* starts out in the DP [$_{DP}$ *there a man*], and it contains the formal features of the DP (see Lasnik 1997; see also Chomsky 1986 and Safir 1982, 1985, 1987 for earlier versions that share some similarities with the proposals we are discussing). The probe enters into Agree with the ϕ-features of the DP, and movement raises the carrier of the ϕ-features—the expletive—to the probe, thereby establishing a PGU at transfer. What is of interest here is that an expletive always starts out with the associate DP, and it undergoes movement, just like a DP. From this standpoint, the expletive construction is not an exception to the need of the goal to move to the probe. Hence, the Moro/Sabel approach allows us to unify all agreement-induced movement, including movement of expletives, as the need of the goal to move to the probe to attain PGU.[3]

Why does *there* split from the rest of its phrase and move? One possible answer is that PGU requires movement; this movement targets the entity that contains the interpretable feature; and in the expletive construction, it is the expletive that has interpretable features. The expletive is morphologically independent of the rest of phrase, so it is able to move without having to pied-pipe the rest. In a normal construction where a full DP moves, the element that carries the interpretable feature (N or D) cannot split from the rest, so the entire DP must pied-pipe to the probe.

Does the expletive raise from the associate that is in its original position? It appears that the associate itself first undergoes movement to a position in the vicinity of v, something reminiscent of the family of proposals that view the internal argument as having to undergo short movement as in (11) (see Johnson 1991, Koizumi 1995, Lasnik 1999b, Runner 1995, Tanaka 1999).

(11) *Short movement of the associate DP*

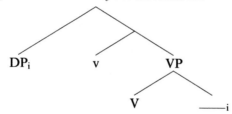

Evidence that this movement occurs comes from the ordering of the DP and the passive participle (Burzio 1986:154–158).

(12) a. There've been some men arrested.
     b. *There've been arrested some men.

The DP, *some men*, must occur before the past participle. Lasnik (1995) argues that this demonstrates movement of the DP to a higher position. The internal argument in an active sentence occurs after the verb in English. To keep the picture consistent, let us assume, following the studies cited earlier, that the internal argument moves to a higher position as in (12a) in all cases, and that the difference between the passive and the active comes from the height of the verb: the passive participle stays low in the structure, while the active verb moves up.

There is evidence for this. As mentioned by Caponigro and Schütze (2003), Blight (1999), using Bowers's (1993) observations about degree-of-perfection adverbs, notes that such adverbs may occur before a passive participle but not after an active participle.

(13) a.   The house was poorly built.
     b.   *They (have) poorly built the house.
     c.   They (have) built the house poorly.

The idea here is that, whereas the passive participle stays low, possibly in its original position, the active participle in (13c) moves up higher across the adverb and also the raised object. Let us assume that in the typical expletive construction involving an unaccusative predicate, the associate DP raises, and the verb then raises above this associate DP, giving the surface form *there V DP*. Under this assumption, the expletive would be launched in examples such as (13a) from a position adjoined to v.

(14)

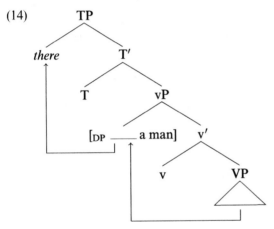

An advantage of the "D" analysis of the expletive is that, as Sabel (2000) argues, it can account for the definiteness effect observed in the expletive construction (Milsark 1974).

(15) There appear(s) *the boy/*every boy/a boy/two boys in the picture.

The associate remains within the nuclear scope, forcing it to have an indefinite reading (Diesing 1992).

    The analysis also provides a straightforward account of an example that Bošković (2002:191) presents in favor of his Case approach to expletives.

(16) *There seems there to be someone in the garden.

Bošković correctly notes that if the only requirement that must be met is that of the EPP on T, externally merging the expletive in the lower (and the matrix) clause should be possible. He argues that the lower Spec,TP is not a Case position, and because Case is settled for the nominal phrase *someone*, nothing should happen in the lower Spec,TP aside from the normal external Merge. On the "D" approach to the expletive, there is no way to derive (16) because there is a one-to-one relation between an expletive and its associate—yet (16) has two expletives for the one associate *someone*.

There is, then, good evidence for the "D" account of the expletive. On this account, the expletive carries the ɸ-features that enter into Agree with the ɸ-probe, making the expletive the target of movement. The "EPP" effect is not one of Case; rather, it arises from the need of the goal to move to the probe.[4]

2.5 The Resumptive Strategy

Danish and Swedish exhibit the *that-t* effect, as shown by the Danish example (17a). Interestingly, the two languages have a repair strategy that is consistent with the analysis of the expletive just presented. (Examples (17a–b) are from Jacobsen and Jensen 1982.)

(17) a. *Vennen   [(som) han pastod [at havde lant]   bogen]]
        friend-DEF C   he claimed C had   borrowed book-DEF
        var forsvundet.
        was disappeared
        'The friend that he claimed had borrowed the book had disappeared.'
    b. Vennen   [(som) han pastod [at *der*   havde lant]
        friend-DEF C   he claimed C there had   borrowed
        bogen]]   var forsvundet.
        book-DEF was disappeared
        'The friend that he claimed had borrowed the book had disappeared.'

In (17b), the *that-t* effect is mitigated by the presence of the expletive *der* in Spec,TP. Given my approach to probe-goal relations, the *that-t* effect in (17a) suggests that the subject *wh*-operator is unable to move to the embedded Spec,TP when *at* 'that' occupies C, a point that must be stipulated. As a result, PGU does not take place at the point where the TP is transferred, which leads to ungrammaticality. Otherwise, a copy of the goal would be left in Spec,TP, and PGU would hold with this copy when the TP is transferred. Based on this, the proposed analysis provides an account of (17b): the expletive acts as a proxy for the goal, just as we saw for the expletive in English, and attains PGU with the probe on T by moving to Spec,TP. The subject *wh*-operator is able to move directly from a lower position to Spec,CP—a phenomenon well documented in Italian (Rizzi 1982). A similar phenomenon occurs in Swedish, except that what acts as the proxy is a resumptive pronoun (Engdahl 1985:8).

(18) a. *Villet ord   visste ingen   [hur ____ staves]?
           which word knew no.one c   is.spelled
           'Which word did no one know how (it) is spelled?'
     b. Villet ord$_i$ visste ingen   [hur *det*$_i$ staves]?
           which word knew no.one c   3SG is.spelled
           'Which word$_i$ did no one know how it$_i$ is spelled?'

Like Danish, Swedish exhibits the *that-t* effect, as shown in (18a). In (18b), the *that-t* effect is mitigated by the occurrence of the resumptive pronoun *det* in the lower Spec,TP. If the analysis proposed here is on the right track, it suggests a direction for analyzing the *that-t* effect in English.[5] We would need to derive the stipulation that when *that* occurs, the subject *wh*-phrase somehow cannot move to Spec,TP.[6]

2.6   *Pro*-Drop

As we have seen, the goal moves to establish a local relation with the probe. So far, all examples of this movement but one have been of category XP—for instance, the external argument moving to Spec,TP. The one exception is movement of the expletive. Under the bare phrase structure approach to structure building, we predict that a goal ought to be able to value a probe by moving directly to the head that contains the probe. We find exactly this configuration in the so-called *pro*-drop languages of Romance and other language families. Because the goal moves to the head that contains the probe, the goal itself must be a head, and the movement responsible for attaining PGU is head movement. Otherwise, all the details of PGU remain the same as in cases of movement to the specifier that we have looked at so far. The *pro*-drop facts are well known. I will just summarize them briefly to show that my proposed system predicts the *pro*-drop phenomenon as reported in the literature.

2.6.1   Romance
In many languages of the world, the subject position may be left empty if the referent is clearly understood from the discourse. This is the *pro*-drop phenomenon, common in Romance languages, but also widespread in many other language families.

(19) *Spanish*
    ____ baila   bien.
    dance.3SG well
    'She dances well.'

(20) *Italian*
    ____ verrà.
    come.3SG.FUT
    'He will come.'

It has long been noted that *pro*-drop languages, at least of the Romance type, have rich inflection (Jespersen 1924, Perlmutter 1971, Rizzi 1978, Taraldsen 1978). In their study of the *pro*-drop phenomenon in Romance and related languages, Alexiadou and Anagnostopoulou (1998) make the important observation that *pro*-drop is actually licensed by *two* factors, rich agreement and a new factor they bring to light.

(21) *Two necessary factors for* pro-*drop (of the Romance type)*
    a. Rich agreement
    b. V-to-T movement, where the agreement shows up on T

Alexiadou and Anagnostopoulou demonstrate the rich agreement requirement with Greek, a typical *pro*-drop language.

(22)

English		*Greek*	
I love	we love	aga*po*	agap*ame*
you love	you love	agap*as*	agap*ate*
he loves	we love	agap*a*	agap*ane*

Unlike English, Greek has unique agreement forms for number and person for each of the six possibilities shown. In addition, as Alexiadou and Anagnostopoulou show, this rich agreement, which appears as inflection on the verb, must occur on T, which is accomplished by the bare verb raising to the richly inflected T. According to Alexiadou and Anagnostopoulou, the rich inflection is a pronominal with a D feature, and it is capable of checking the EPP feature on T, which they assume is a D feature on T, following Chomsky (1995). The pronominal agreement on T takes care of the EPP/D requirement, with the result that nothing needs to move to Spec,TP. In fact, on Alexiadou and Anagnostopoulou's analysis, Spec,TP is never filled in Greek or any of the other *pro*-drop languages, since the EPP feature on T is independently checked by the rich agreement. I will return to this issue of V-to-T movement later.

Under the approach I am pursuing, the analysis of *pro*-drop would be essentially the same as Alexiadou and Anagnostopoulou's. A head that contains "rich" interpretable φ-features—the goal—occurs in the grammatical subject position, and the φ-probe at T enters into an Agree relation with it. Subsequently, the goal moves to the φ-probe by head raising, thereby establishing a PGU. The requirement that V move to T presumably exists to morphologically support the agreement head at T.

Alexiadou and Anagnostopoulou's system predicts that there is nothing in Spec,TP in *pro*-drop languages—an account I would concur with because the goal in the form of the agreement head raises to T.[7] There are, however, instances where a subject occurs preverbally. Alexiadou and Anagnostopoulou note that preverbal subjects have a special interpretation, something akin to a "topic," which suggests that they occupy a higher, Ā-position. Accordingly, Alexiadou and Anagnostopoulou analyze the preverbal subject in this way (example from 1998:506).

(23) SVO: S is not in Spec,TP in Greek/Romance
    Indefinite preverbal subject: strong (partitive/specific) reading
    a. Ena pedhi diavase to   "Paramithi horis Onoma."
       a   child read   the "Fairy Tale without a Title"
       'A certain child/One of the children read "Fairy Tale without a Title."'
    b. Diavase ena pedhi to "Paramithi horis Onoma."
       'One of the children read "Fairy Tale without a Title."'

The preverbal indefinite 'a child' in (23a) has a partitive/specific reading, whereas the postverbal subject in (23b) may receive a nonspecific interpretation.

Finally, another typical property of *pro*-drop languages is what is called "subject inversion."

(24) *Subject inversion in Romance*
    a. Ha   mangiato   Giovanni.   (Italian)
    b. Ha   comida   Juan.   (Spanish)
       have.3SG eat.PART.PAST John
       'John has eaten.'

The "inverted subject" never occupied Spec,TP because it never functions as the goal of the probe; hence, it can occur in the "inverted" position to begin with or be moved there from some lower position (Kenstowicz 1989, Rizzi 1982).

2.6.2 Bani-Hassan Arabic

In discussing φ-feature agreement, I have abstracted away from the different types of agreement and their role in movement. I will continue to do this to keep the exposition focused on movement and related matters. However, it is important to note for the record that there is a rich literature on person, number, and gender agreements, with an apparent consensus building that person appears always to function as "true" agreement whereas number and gender sometimes do not manifest all the expected properties of genuine agreement (e.g., Baker 2008, Boeckx 2007, Ouhalla 2005, Sigurðsson 2007). One example of this is found in Bani-Hassan, an Arabic dialect spoken by "a Bedouin clan of the Jordanian desert" (Kenstowicz 1989:264). According to Kenstowicz (1989:272), this language has the following inflections:

(25) a. +tense, +person finite
   b. −tense, +person subjunctive
   c. +tense, −person participle

Quoting Kenstowicz (1989:272–273):

Finite verbs exhibit independent selection for the categories of tense/aspect. They may thus appear in main clauses as well as in *innu* 'that' clauses complement to verbs such as *gaal* 'say', *iʕtigad* 'think', etc. Subjunctive denotes verbs that exhibit no independent selection for tense/aspect but nevertheless show full obligatory agreement with the subject.... The participle ... only shows distinctions in gender (masculine versus feminine) and number (singular and plural).

Kenstowicz goes on to show that the participial inflection does not allow *pro*-drop of the subject, unlike the forms with +person; see (26), from Kenstowicz 1989:265–266. This suggests that a head that can function as the goal of a probe must have person agreement. (In some languages, that is not sufficient; Holmberg (2005) notes that in Finnish, first- and second-person agreement license *pro*-drop but third-person agreement does not.)

(26) a. *Finite form*
       Al-binit gaalat innu ____ ištarat al-libaas.
       the-girl said   that   bought the-dress
     b. *Participle*
       Fariid gaal *innu/inn-ha mištarya al-libaas.
       Fariid said that/that-she bought   the-dress

Kenstowicz also notes that the finite form has the typical *pro*-drop property of subject inversion that we observed in Romance and Greek, but the participle does not allow it. This indicates that in the participial construction, the fully specified DP subject functions as the goal that must be raised to Spec,TP to attain PGU.

(27) a. *Finite form (uninverted)*
       Fariid gaal innu al-binit ištarat al-libaas.
       Fariid said that the-girl bought the-dress
     b. *Finite form (inverted)*
       Fariid gaal innu ištarat al-binit al-libaas.
       Fariid said that bought the-girl the-dress

(28) a. *Participle (uninverted)*
       Fariid gaal innu al-binit mištarya al-libaas.
       Fariid said that the-girl bought   the-dress
     b. *Participle (inverted)*
       *Fariid gaal innu mištarya al-binit al-libaas.
       Fariid said that bought   the-girl the-dress

2.7   Chinese as an Agreement Language

In this section, I will suggest that Chinese is an agreement language that patterns in many ways like the *pro*-drop languages we looked at in the previous section.[8] This is different from the usual view of Chinese as a topic-prominent language. This topic prominence is illustrated in (29).

(29) *Zhe-ben shu*   Zhangsan mai-le.
     this-CL   book Zhangsan buy-ASP
     'This book, Zhangsan bought.'

It is generally believed that the topic in (29) occupies a position higher than Spec,TP. From the present perspective this means that the topic feature remains at C, in turn suggesting that only the ϕ-probe is inherited by T, giving rise to an agreement language. I propose that Chinese shares relevant features along these lines with agreement languages such as Romance and Bani-Hassan Arabic—in particular, the idea that person agreement at T licenses *pro*-drop.

Word order in Chinese is typically SVO, and adverbial modifiers occur between the subject and the object.

(30) Zhangsan zuotian   zai xuexiao kanjian-le Lisi.
     Zhangsan yesterday at   school see-ASP   Lisi
     'Zhangsan saw Lisi at school yesterday.'

One exception to SVO order is found in the *ba* construction, where the object occurs preverbally, accompanied by *ba*.

(31) a. Ta pian-le   Lisi.
      he cheat-ASP Lisi
      'He cheated Lisi.'
    b. Ta ba Lisi pian-le.
      he BA Lisi cheat-ASP
      'He cheated Lisi.'

In the *ba* sentence in (31b), focus is placed on the *ba* phrase; and in certain cases, the presence of the *ba* phrase changes the aspectual interpretation (see, e.g., Li 1990, Li and Thompson 1981, Tenny 1994).

If we are to argue for an analysis that involves person agreement at T in Chinese, like the analyses proposed for Romance and other *pro*-drop languages, we first must establish that there is, in fact, a T projection in this language. Because there is no T projection that can be identified, many linguists have suggested that Chinese does not have T (see references in Sybesma 2007). In contrast, Sybesma (2007) and Tang (1998) provide arguments that it does have T. The examples and discussion are from Sybesma 2007:581 (I omit diacritics for tones, following the practice of other linguists).

The pair of examples in (32) appear to indicate that there is no T in Chinese.

(32) a. Zhangsan zhu zai zher.
      Zhangsan live at here
      'Zhangsan lives here.'
    b. Zhangsan 1989 nian zhu zai zher.
      Zhangsan 1989 year live at here
      'Zhangsan lived here in 1989.'

Example (32a) has a present tense interpretation, but when '1989 year' is added as in (32b), the interpretation is that of past tense. On the face of it, this appears to indicate that Chinese does not have tense and that the interpretation 'past' comes about with the inclusion of a temporal phrase like '1989' (similarly for other temporal interpretations). However, Sybesma notes, following Matthewson (2002), that this is the wrong way to view the pair in (32). Specifically, he points out that (32a) has a present tense interpretation. Where would this interpretation come from if Chinese has no tense? It is truly a present tense interpretation because, for example, if the subject refers to a person who is dead, the sentence is nonsensical. (See Sybesma 2007 for other arguments.)

Now, if the T projection indeed occurs in Chinese, where is it located? Because there is no overt manifestation of T as far as we can see, we have to locate it through indirect means. There are two considerations here. First, the aspectual marker *le* occurs in mid-sentence, and it is often the case that an aspectual marker occurs in the proximity of tense, as in Japanese. Second, if Chinese is indeed a *pro*-drop language like those discussed in section 2.6, verb raising should raise the verb to T (Alexiadou and Anagnostopoulou 1998). The verb in fact occurs in mid-sentence, next to *le*. Let us, then, suppose that T occurs in Chinese in a position similar to the one it occupies in English and Romance. If we look again at the examples that contain an overt subject, and in particular at where this subject occurs relative to T, we see that while it appears to occur next to T in some cases, it can also occur away from T, as when an adjunct (30) or the *ba* phrase in a *ba* construction (31b) intervenes. This is expected under the *pro*-drop analysis because the overt subject is not the goal of the probe at T; instead, the goal is the agreement head, so the overt phrase corresponding to the subject is free to occur away from T.[9]

The next step is to establish that *pro* may occur in subject position but nowhere else—something that turns out to be a challenge in Chinese because, unlike Romance, Chinese is a massively *pro*-drop language, allowing gaps not only in subject position but also in, for example, object position. Fortunately, C.-T. J. Huang (1984) has established that the gap in subject position is *pro*, whereas the gap in object position is a variable created by Ā-movement of an empty topic.

(33) Zhangsan shuo [*e* bu renshi Lisi].
      Zhangsan say   *e* not know Lisi
      'Zhangsan said that [he] did not know Lisi.'

(34) Zhangsan shuo [Lisi bu renshi *e*].
      Zhangsan say   Lisi not know *e*
      'Zhangsan said that Lisi did not know [him].'

Example (33) contains a subject gap in the subordinate clause, and (34) an object gap. Huang observes that the subject gap in (33) can refer either to the matrix subject *Zhangsan* or to someone else in the discourse. In contrast, the object gap in (34) can only refer to someone else in the discourse, not to the matrix subject. Huang accounts for this asymmetry between subject and object gaps by proposing that the subject gap is a *pro* that can refer either to the matrix subject or to someone else in the discourse. The object gap in (34) is instead a variable bound by a null discourse topic that begins in the subordinate object position and undergoes Ā-movement to the topic position in the matrix clause.[10] This means that, in Chinese, the topic feature stays at C, and if the line we are pursuing in this section is correct, the φ-probe in the form of a person feature is inherited by T. Further evidence for the subject/object asymmetry shows up in topicalization, which involves a potential Crossover violation (C.-T. J. Huang 1984:558).

(35) a. Zhangsan$_i$, ta$_i$ shuo [e_i mei kanjian Lisi].
         Zhangsan he say e no see   Lisi
         'Zhangsan$_i$, he$_i$ said that [he$_i$] didn't see Lisi.'
     b. *Zhangsan$_i$, ta$_i$ shuo [Lisi mei kanjian e_i].
         Zhangsan he say   Lisi no see e
         'Zhangsan$_i$, he$_i$ said that Lisi didn't see [him$_i$].'

The topicalized *Zhangsan* in (35a) is coreferential with the subordinate subject, whereas the one in (35b) is coreferential with the subordinate object. Huang notes that (35a) is grammatical, presumably because the subordinate subject is *pro*—hence, no movement has occurred to produce topicalization, and a Crossover violation is thereby avoided. By contrast, (35b) is ungrammatical because the subordinate object gap has a variable created by Ā-movement of the topic—movement that triggers a Strong Crossover violation.

As we have seen, Sybesma's (2007) work (also Tang 1998) establishes the possibility that Chinese has a tense projection, and C.-T. J. Huang's (1984) work on subject and object gaps shows that the subject gap is *pro* but the object gap is created by movement. To argue that Chinese is an agreement language, we also have to show that Chinese does in fact evidence φ-feature agreement associated with the subject. We can do this by looking at what is called the "blocking effect" for the reflexive anaphor *ziji* (Y.-H. Huang 1984, Tang 1985, 1989). As (36) shows, *ziji* can function as a long-distance anaphor across a more local potential antecedent. (All examples in this discussion of the blocking effect are taken from Pan 2000.)

(36) Zhangsan$_i$ zhidao Lisi$_j$ dui ziji$_{i/j}$ mei xinxin.
     Zhangsan know Lisi to self   not confidence
     'Zhangsan knows that Lisi has no confidence in him/himself.'

Note that in this example, both matrix and subordinate subjects are third person. However, if the potential antecedent in the next higher clause does not match the lower potential antecedent in person, the long-distance construal of *ziji* is blocked, leaving only the local subject as its antecedent.

(37) a. Wo$_i$ juede ni$_j$ dui ziji-$_{*i/j}$ mei xinxin.
          I   think you to self   not confidence
          'I think you have no confidence in yourself/*me.'
      b. Ni$_i$ juede wo$_j$ dui ziji-$_{*i/j}$ mei xinxin   ma?
          you think I   to self   not confidence Q
          'Do you think I have no confidence in myself/*you?'
      c. Zhangsan$_i$ juede wo/ni$_j$ dui ziji-$_{i/j}$ mei xinxin.
          Zhangsan think I/you to self   not confidence
          'Zhangsan thinks I/you have no confidence in myself/yourself/
          *him.'

In these examples, the matrix and subordinate subjects do not match in
person ((37a): first-second; (37b): second-first; (37c): third-first/second).
This mismatch blocks *ziji* from long-distance construal. This blocking effect has been given as evidence that a subject-oriented anaphor undergoes
movement at LF (e.g., Battistella 1989, Cole, Hermon, and Sung 1990,
Huang and Tang 1991). One implementation consistent with the idea
that there is person agreement at T in Chinese is that *ziji* raises to its local
T, where it takes on the person value of the T (the person feature already
valued by the subject phrase). *Ziji* can, then, move to T in the higher
clause, and if the person feature on that T matches the person feature
already on *ziji*, long-distance construal is possible. This, or some other
approach, requires the existence of a person feature in Chinese.[11]

A point worth making here, though, is that Japanese does not exhibit
the blocking effect.

(38) Taroo/Watakusi/Anata-wa [Taroo/watakusi/anata-ga zibun-no
      Taro/I/you-TOP   Taro/I/you-NOM   self-GEN
      syasin-o   totta to] itta.
      picture-ACC take C   said
      'Taro/I/You said that Taro/I/you took self's picture.'

Setting aside a certain pragmatic awkwardness with some possible interpretations, it is possible in principle for the anaphor to refer to the subordinate or matrix subject in any combination. This indicates that the
anaphor in Japanese is sensitive to subjects but not to person agreement.

Recall that in the *pro*-drop languages we looked at in section 2.6, a
verb-initial order with postverbal "subject" is possible. Although such a
sequence is apparently not as common in Chinese, we do find examples
like (39) and (40), taken from Huang 1982.

(39) Yu xia-guo le.
rain fall-ASP ASP
'It has rained.'

(40) Xia-guo le   yu   le.
fall-ASP ASP rain ASP
'It has rained.'

As a reviewer notes, the question remains why Chinese does not easily allow the verb-subject order found in Romance.

Finally, the *pro*-drop analysis may account for a mystery about quantifier scope. In Chinese, two quantifiers in a simple clause are limited to surface scope; inverse scope is not possible. This was noted originally for Japanese by Kuroda (1971), and Huang (1982:113) discovered that the same fact holds in Chinese.

(41) Youyige xuesheng bu mai suoyonde shu.
one   student   not buy all   book
'There was a student who did not buy all the books (only some).'

(42) Meige xuesheng dou mai-le   yiben shu.
every student   all buy-ASP one book
'For every student x, there is one book y such that x bought y.'

A possible explanation is that the subject, which is not the goal, occurs in a position higher than TP, most likely a topic position. Recall Alexiadou and Anagnostopoulou's (1998) Greek example (43), which has only surface scope.

(43) Ena pedhi diavase to "Paramithi horis Onoma."
a   child read   the "Fairy Tale without a Title"
'A certain child/One of the children read "Fairy Tale without a Title."'

The reason for the lack of ambiguity is that 'a child' here is not the true subject, and it occurs in a higher position (Alexiadou and Anagnostopoulou claim that it is an Ā-position, but we will see in chapter 3 that at least the comparable position in Japanese is best analyzed as an A-position).

If what I have proposed in this section is on the right track and Chinese has person agreement, why doesn't it ever appear as verbal inflection, as in other agreement languages? There is no simple answer to this; rather, a combination of factors leads to this unusual situation. First, it appears that Chinese noun phrases are unable to value a probe; in other words, the noun phrases do not have interpretable agreement features. Why would this be the case? We might speculate as follows, on the basis of a proposal by Chierchia (1998). Chierchia argues for two types of nominal expressions: those, like English and Romance nominals, that can refer to individuals; and those, like Chinese nominals (and he specifically discusses Chinese), that refer to kinds. It could be that the English-type nominal expressions are DPs and that D is typically the locus of φ-feature agreement (although it isn't clear why); and that the Chinese-type expressions are NPs, which would be unable to host φ-features, so they don't. On the other hand, given the *pro*-drop nature of Chinese, and following the analysis of Romance, we can speculate that the "small *pro*" in Chinese does have an interpretable feature—specifically, a person feature—and it is this feature that enters into an Agree relation with the φ-probe. The *pro* then moves to the probe for PGU, and its phonetically empty nature leads to a lack of verbal agreement inflection.

But then, how can the language learner ever figure out that Chinese has person agreement? Here, speculating again, and reflecting on the spirit of the Uniformity Principle (Chomsky 2001), interpreted here as Strong Uniformity, we might say that in the absence of any overt indication of agreement, and in the absence of any indication that the language is of the topic/focus type, where topic/focus is inherited by T, the language learner simply turns to the default universal setting for agreement. This φ-feature agreement must be inherited by T. Given that there is no indication that the nominal can provide valuation, the language learner assumes that an agreement head, which happens to be unpronounced, provides the valuation. Finally, in the absence of overt manifestation of φ-features, the learner assumes the most basic form of agreement—namely, person agreement. Other explanations exist, but whatever one might come up with, it must account for the sheer lack of overt manifestation of φ-features in the inflectional system combined with a clear manifestation of person agreement in the construal of the anaphor *ziji*.

2.8   Irish

VSO languages call into question the idea of PGU. Irish is one such language. (All examples are from McCloskey 2001.)

(44) Do   fuair sé nuachtán Meiriceánach óna   dheartháir
     PAST got   he newspaper American   from.his brother
     an lá cheana.
     the-other-day
     'He got an American paper from his brother the other day.'

McCloskey (1996) originally argued that the subject is in VP and that the EPP is inactive in Irish. For the sentence in (45), he postulated the structure in (46).

(45) D' ól   sí depcj uisce.
     PAST drink she drink water
     'She drank a drink of water.'

(46)

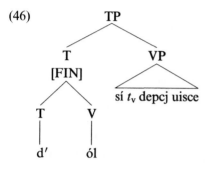

In (46), there is no way for PGU to obtain because the subject remains in VP. However, McCloskey has since argued that the subject raises to a "subject" position next to T (McCloskey 2001). From the perspective taken here, this means that T Case-marks the subject, and the φ-probe at T is valued by the subject, which then moves to a position in the projection of T for the purpose of establishing a PGU. McCloskey (2001:169) characterizes this position as a "nominative" position and a "subject" position. The process McCloskey proposes is similar to the raising of the agreement morpheme to T in *pro*-drop languages, except that what has moved is a DP. As one piece of evidence, McCloskey gives the following periphrastic progressive aspect sentences:

(47) a. Tá ag   neartú ar a ghlór.
      is strengthen PROG on his voice
      'His voice is strengthening.'
    b. Tá a ghlór ag   neartú.
      is his voice strengthen PROG
      'His voice is strengthening.'

In (47a), the complement is a PP ('on his voice'), but in (47b), it is a bare DP ('his voice'). As shown, the PP in (47a) stays low, presumably in VP, while the bare DP in (47b) raises above the progressive verb, which suggests that it occupies a position in the vicinity of T. The φ-probe on T is appropriately valued, and PGU has taken place as required.

2.9 A Word about Long-Distance Agreement

I need to say something about the so-called long-distance agreement (LDA) reported in a variety of languages (e.g., Hindi-Urdu: Mahajan 1989, Bhatt 2005; Itelmen: Bobaljik and Wurmbrand 2005; Tsez: Polinsky and Potsdam 2001). Typical LDA has the form exemplified by the Hindi-Urdu sentence (48a) from Mahajan 1989:234:

(48) a. Ram-ne [roṭii   khaa-nii] chaah-ii.
        Ram-ERG bread.F eat-INF.F want-PVF.FSG
        'Ram wanted to eat bread.'
     b. Ram-ne [roṭii   khaa-naa] chaah-aa.
        Ram-ERG bread.F eat-INF.M want-PVF.MSG
        'Ram wanted to eat bread.'

In (48a), the matrix verbal inflection agrees with the object 'bread' in the infinitival, and this agreement also shows up on the infinitival. This LDA is optional, and when it does not occur, as in (48b), the matrix inflection takes on the default masculine singular, and the infinitival does not inflect for agreement. Mahajan (1989) analyzes the LDA in Hindi-Urdu in a way that is consistent with the PGU—that is, despite the appearance of LDA, PGU for ϕ-features is needed here. In his account, the object in the infinitival clause first undergoes movement within the infinitival, where it enters into agreement with the infinitival verbal complex. It then moves to the matrix clause, to the position Mahajan identifies as Spec,AgrP. By moving in this way, the embedded object, which functions as the goal of the ϕ-probe, moves to the probe and establishes a PGU.

Bobaljik and Wurmbrand (2005) propose a similar account for LDA in Itelmen. They show, among other things, that when the embedded object enters into LDA, it must take matrix scope, whereas when it does not, it is limited to being interpreted inside the infinitival (Bobaljik and Wurmbrand 2005:849).

These views of LDA are promising for PGU, but challenges remain. Bhatt (2005) proposes an alternative account of the Hindi-Urdu facts that does not necessarily involve movement of the subordinate object. And in Tsez, the embedded object that apparently functions as the goal of the ϕ-probe in the matrix clause may be preceded by other elements in the infinitive, as shown in (49) (Polinsky and Potsdam 2001:584).

(49) enir   [užā magalu   bāc'ruli] b-iyxo.
     mother boy bread.III.ABS ate.IV   III-know
     'The mother knows (that) the boy ate the bread.'

The embedded object 'bread' agrees with the matrix verbal complex. Note that this object is preceded by the subordinate subject 'boy', which makes a simple movement analysis of the embedded object to the matrix clause implausible. Polinsky and Potsdam do note that the embedded object that enters into LDA has a "topic" interpretation, and they in fact argue that the object undergoes movement to the subordinate topic position in the CP domain. This argument is still not sufficient to overcome the difficulty this example poses, however, given that the goal is still in the subordinate structure; and besides, if Polinsky and Potsdam are right, the movement only occurs at LF. I will leave these problems for future study.[12]

2.10 A Brief Look Back at West Flemish

As the last item to be discussed in this chapter, let us go back to an issue from chapter 1. Recall the West Flemish examples that show complementizer agreement as well as subject-verb agreement (from Carstens 2003, based on Haegeman 1992).

(50) a. Kpeinzen *dan-k* (ik) morgen   goan.
        I.think   that-I (I) tomorrow go
        'I think that I'll go tomorrow.'
     b. Kpeinzen *da-j*   (gie) morgen   goat.
        I.think   that-you (you) tomorrow go
        'I think that you'll go tomorrow.'
     c. Kvinden *dan*   die boeken te   diere   zyn.
        I.find   that.PL the books too expensive are
        'I find those books too expensive.'

The problem is that we assume that a φ-probe does not undergo valuation until it is inherited by T or a related head where some mechanism is available for the φ-probe to identify its goal. This assumption predicts that a φ-probe at C should not undergo valuation. However, the complementizer agreement makes it seem as though not only does a copy of the φ-probe remain on C, but in fact this copy can seek a goal on its own without the help of an activation mechanism such as Case. But the problem is in fact more complex. As Van Koppen (2006) and others point out, the complementizer agreement and the agreement on the verbal inflection do not always match. A particularly striking example is (51), from Bavarian (Van Koppen 2006:3).

(51) a. ...dass-ds   du   und d'Maria   an Hauptpreis gwunna
          that-2PL [you.SG and the Maria]2PL the first.prize   won
          hab-ds.
          have-2PL
     b. ...dass-sd   du   und d'Maria   an Hauptpreis gwunna
          that-2SG [you.SG and the Maria]2PL the first.prize   won
          hab-ds.
          have-2PL
          '...that you and Maria have won the first prize.'

In (51a), the complementizer and the verbal inflection match, both showing second person plural, which agrees with the subject. The interesting
fact is (51b), where the complementizer agrees with the first conjunct by
inflecting for singular, while the verbal agreement is plural. Van Koppen
proposes that the φ-probe starts at C and is inherited by T, but that a
copy of the φ-probe remains at C. The two φ-probes then undergo valuation independently, although each picks out the subject as its goal. Although the verbal agreement always agrees with the full goal phrase, the
complementizer is able to agree with a feature that is a subcomponent of
the subject phrase.

   Note that on this kind of analysis, we cannot assume the phase-based
approach to agreement for complementizer agreement. Although the subject and the φ-probe on T represent a typical agreement configuration,
complementizer agreement does not. From Van Koppen's data involving
first-conjunct agreement, it appears that in complementizer agreement,
the probe-goal relation is established strictly through string adjacency, of
the type familiar in phrasal phonology (e.g., Archangeli and Pulleyblank
1987, Odden 1994, Steriade 1987). The copy of the φ-probe at C is not
valued in narrow syntax; instead, the valuation takes place at PF, after
the phases have been put back together, and the complementizer and the
subject are string adjacent. Chomsky (2007) suggests that complementizer
agreement is concordance, not agreement, which possibly points to the
same conclusion: that it is a PF phenomenon. Semantics—or, for that
matter, information structure—does not interpret this agreement because
the agreement relation only holds at PF. This, I believe, is correct: the relevant functional relation is between the subject and T. Although complementizer agreement appears to be fundamentally different in this way, it
is important to note that, under my analysis, which is based on Van Koppen's work, the idea that the φ-probe begins at C still stands. Complementizer agreement is a residue of this φ-probe at C.

As the final note, if the proposed analysis is on the right track, we would expect not only the subject to occur adjacent to the complementizer, but also the expletive, since we are assuming that the expletive is a proxy for the goal. Consider the following West Flemish example, pointed out to me by Liliane Haegeman:

(52) ... dan/*da   der morgen   meer studenten goan kommen.
     that.PL/*that.SG there tomorrow more students   go   come
     '... that there will be coming more students tomorrow.'

The expletive *der* occurs adjacent to the complementizer, as we would expect. Also presumably so that it can be adjacent to the complementizer, the expletive occurs to the left of the time adverbial *morgen* 'tomorrow'. The following example, also pointed out to me by Liliane Haegeman, demonstrates the same point:

(53) ... dan/*da   der dienen boek nie vee   studenten kennen.
     that.PL/*that.SG there that   book not many students   know
     '... that not many students know that book.'

The object has been moved to the left of the subject, possibly for reasons of topicalization, and the expletive *der* occurs to the left of this object and adjacent to the complementizer.[13]

This discussion also pertains to a problem I have ignored so far: the problem of auxiliary inversion in English *wh*-questions.

(54) What does John want?

The auxiliary, *does*, is at C, but its goal, *John*, is in Spec,TP. *Does* and *John* are not adjacent according to our account based on the bare phrase structure approach. However, they are *string* adjacent. So, whatever the reason for auxiliary inversion—possibly the same as the one given above for the Bavarian and West Flemish phenomena: that there is a copy of the ϕ-feature at C that must be valued—its placement at C need not be viewed as violating the PGU requirement. It is just that in this case, the PGU requirement would hold at PF only.

2.11 Summary

In this chapter, I offered a reason why movement exists in natural language. Movement plays a critical role in enhancing the expressive power of language, although the way movement works is intricate enough that its function is not immediately obvious. Movement of the type we have looked at—A-movement triggered by a grammatical feature that starts at C and is inherited by T—is a record of functional relations. A functional relation is established by Agree, but if nothing else happens, the record of this critical relation is erased before semantic interpretation and interpretation for information structure because the probe must be deleted. Natural language has figured out a way to tap the expressive power of functional relations by installing an intricate system of agreement, which includes φ-features and topic/focus, and instituting the process of valuation. Movement forces the goal to move to the probe to retain a record of the functional relations. I called this *probe-goal union*.

A look at constructions in a number of languages, including mitigation of the *that-t* effect, *pro*-drop, and VSO word order, revealed that the goal that values the probe may be an XP or a head, either being possible because of the notions inherent to the bare phrase structure approach on which I built my arguments about movement. One language discussed here, Chinese, poses an interesting question. Because it has no agreement morphology, it has generally been considered to be a topic-prominent language. But it gives evidence for φ-feature agreement in the form of person features even though it lacks person agreement morphology. How can the language learner figure out that this language has person agreement? As one possibility, I speculated that, given the approach that every language has φ-feature agreement, the language learner simply assumes the basic universal—that is, initial-state—agreement, which would be just person agreement.

I briefly discussed three additional issues. The first was surface VSO word order in Irish, which seemingly contradicts the PGU requirement because the subject could be viewed as staying in vP. However, McCloskey's work shows that the subject in fact moves to a position close to T, and we can assume that this movement satisfies the PGU requirement. The second issue was long-distance agreement, which appears to blatantly violate the adjacency requirement for agreement. I noted some analyses that propose that the embedded object moves to the matrix clause, which would make this phenomenon compatible with PGU, but there are problems that remain for future study. The third issue was complementizer agreement. In Bavarian and West Flemish, the agreement on the complementizer is not always identical to the agreement on the verbal inflection. What appears to allow the φ-probe "copy" to be valued at C is string adjacency, something that I speculated might also apply to auxiliary inversion in English *wh*-questions.

3 Unifying A-Movements

3.1 Introduction

In Government-Binding (GB) Theory, A-movement was defined as movement to a "potential" θ-position (Chomsky 1981). The *A* in *A-movement* comes from the idea that a phrase that undergoes this movement moves to a potential argument (A-)position. In virtually all cases, this position is what we today would call Spec,TP. In GB and all its predecessors, it was postulated that Spec,TP is where the external argument of a predicate is assigned. In the sentence *John ate pizza*, *John* merges directly into Spec,TP, where it receives the external θ-role; the source of this argument θ-role is the VP (Marantz 1984). Just in those constructions that do not assign an external θ-role, such as the passive, raising, and unaccusative constructions, Spec,TP becomes available for A-movement. Although no external θ-role is assigned in these cases, Spec,TP is a "potential" position for the external θ-role, and in GB this was sufficient to count it as an argument position for the sake of movement. However, this way of characterizing A-movement became obsolete with the advent of the predicate-internal subject hypothesis (Kuroda 1988, Sportiche 1988; see also Fukui 1986, Kitagawa 1986). This hypothesis postulates that the external θ-role, as well as the internal θ-role, is assigned inside the verbal projection, either VP or vP depending on the version of the hypothesis, so that the external θ-role is never assigned to Spec,TP. This hypothesis, which has gained wide currency, is one of the major features that separate GB and the current Minimalist Program. Obviously, if no θ-role is ever assigned to Spec,TP, this position is never an "A" position as far as θ-roles are concerned, so the idea of characterizing it as a "potential" argument position for movement is no longer an option. How can we portray this position in a way that is consistent with current theory?

One possibility is that the distinction between A-movement and Ā-movement is unnecessary. However, there is good empirical evidence to suggest that these two types of movement do behave differently. A-movement does not trigger a Weak Crossover (WCO) violation, and it can create a new binder (e.g., Mahajan 1990).

(1) Who$_i$ t_i seems to his$_i$ mother t_i to be smart?

(2) John$_i$ seems to himself$_i$ to be t_i smart.

In (1), the *wh*-phrase *who* undergoes A-movement from the subordinate subject position to the matrix Spec,TP, crossing the pronoun *his*. Nevertheless, the sentence is grammatical. A WCO violation is invoked if the sentence contains a variable, and if there is a pronoun coreferential with the variable that the variable fails to c-command. Not being a form of operator movement, A-movement does not create a variable, so in (1) the trace and the pronoun in the subordinate subject position are not subject to WCO. In (2), *John* undergoes A-movement to Spec,TP and is able to bind *himself* from this new position. Presumably, such binding only takes place from A-positions.

By contrast, as (3) and (4) show, Ā-movement is incapable of suppressing a WCO violation; it also cannot create a new binder.

(3) ?*Who$_i$ does his$_i$ mother love t_i?

(4) *To whom$_i$ did Mary introduce each other$_i$'s friends t_i?

How can we define A-movement? If we limit ourselves to English, it is possible to characterize it as movement triggered by the agreement feature on T. In (1) and (2), the phrase that moves into Spec,TP is the so-called goal of the agreement at T, and it is this agreement that marks the goal phrase for movement. The same holds for the typical "EPP" movement of an external argument from Spec,vP to Spec,TP—again, by agreement on T.

(5) *A-movement (tentative)*
    An agreement feature on T targets the goal of the agreement for movement.

However, attempting to define A-movement within the predicate-internal subject hypothesis became complex when Mahajan (1990) identified the same properties discussed above for a certain subtype of scrambling. A typical example of this kind of scrambling is movement of the object to the head of the sentence above the subject. The following Japanese examples are modeled after Mahajan's work, and similar examples are discussed by Hoji (1985), Saito (1992), Tada (1993), and Yoshimura (1989, 1992). As shown, "A" scrambling can suppress a WCO violation.

(6) a. *[Kinoo pro_i pro_j atta hito$_i$]-ga   dare-o$_j$ hihansita no?
        yesterday   met person-NOM who-ACC criticized Q
        Lit. 'The person who met (him) yesterday criticized whom?'
    b. Dare-o$_j$ [kinoo pro_i pro_j atta hito$_i$]-ga t_j hihansita no?
        who-ACC yesterday   met person-NOM   criticized Q
        Lit. 'Who, the person who met (him) yesterday criticized?'

This type of scrambling can also create a new binder (Mahajan 1990, Saito 1992).

(7) a. *Otagai$_i$-no   sensei-ga   [Taroo-to Hanako]$_i$-o
        each.other-GEN teacher-NOM Taro-and Hanako-ACC
        suisensita.
        recommended
        'Each other's teachers recommended Taro and Hanaka.'
    b. Taroo-to Hanako-o$_i$ otagai-no   sensei-ga t_i
        Taro-and Hanako-ACC each.other-GEN teacher-NOM
        suisensita.
        recommended
        'Taro and Hanako, each other's teachers recommended.'

Unlike this kind of local scrambling, long-distance scrambling has solely Ā properties, so that it is unable to suppress a WCO violation and cannot create a new binder (Mahajan 1990, Saito 1992, Tada 1993, Yoshimura 1989, 1992).

(8) *Dare-o$_j$ [kinoo pro_i pro_j atta hito$_i$]-ga
     who-ACC yesterday   met person-NOM
     [Taroo-ga t_j sitteiru to] itta no?
     Taro-NOM   know C   said Q
     Lit. 'Who, the person who met (him) yesterday said that Taro knows (him)?'

(9) ?*Taroo-to Hanako-o$_i$ otagai-no   sensei-ga
     Taro-and Hanako-ACC each.other-GEN teacher-NOM
     [koutyou-ga t_i sikaru to] omotta.
     principal-NOM   scold C   thought
     Lit. 'Taro and Hanako, each other's teachers thought that the principal will scold.'

There is no φ-feature agreement in the relevant scrambling constructions that would enable us to characterize the clearly "A" nature of these movements in the same way that we portrayed English A-movements. Another possible mechanism that Mahajan (1990) suggests is Case, which works for English, where Spec,TP could be viewed as the position to which nominative Case is assigned, though not necessarily. This, too, will not work for A-scrambling, however.

I suggest that, as already noted in chapters 1 and 2, the cases where scrambling can be characterized as A-movement involve a grammatical feature that is computationally equivalent to φ-feature agreement. Following the proposal of É. Kiss (1995, 1997, 2003), I assume that Japanese is a discourse-configurational language and therefore that information-structural notions such as topic and focus are grammaticalized and play the same role in narrow syntax in Japanese that φ-feature agreement plays in agreement languages. In chapter 1, we saw that topic/focus and φ-features begin at C and that in Japanese-type languages, topic/focus lowers to T. In this way, focus occupies the same position—T—as φ-feature agreement and attracts a topic/focus phrase to Spec,TP. A slight change in the tentative definition of A-movement that I gave in (5) covers the scrambling cases.

(10) *A-movement (revised)*
     A grammatical feature on T targets the goal of the agreement for movement.

In chapter 4, I will show that (10), although correct, is simply a description of one type of movement that I have been calling A-movement. As I will show, (10) can be derived from considerations of chain formation within a phase-based architecture of narrow syntax. But first, I need to establish that topic/focus indeed triggers A-movement, which is the task of this chapter. I begin with a discussion of focus.

3.2   Focus Movement as A-Movement to Spec,TP

Japanese has numerous expressions that are associated with focus. We saw in chapter 1 that the indeterminate pronoun provides one piece of evidence for focus movement to Spec,TP. In this section, I take up another type of focus phrase: the *XP-mo* 'XP-also' expression studied by Hasegawa (1991, 1994, 2005) and Kuroda (1965, 1971).

3.2.1 The Japanese 'Also' Phrase

Hasegawa (2005) (see also Miyagawa 2007) has proposed that, just like
the indeterminate pronoun, the *mo* 'also' expression undergoes A-
movement, in most cases to Spec,TP.[1] Here, I will give further evidence
that the movement is indeed A-movement.[2] This will lay the groundwork
for showing that focus in Japanese is a grammatical feature that is comparable to ϕ-feature agreement in agreement languages such as those of
Indo-European, as I argued in chapter 1, thereby further supporting the
analysis of focus as a feature relevant to syntactic movement (e.g., Brody
1990, Horvath 1981, 1986, 1995, É. Kiss 1995). Once I establish that this
focus movement takes place to Spec,TP, I will expand the analysis and
show that there is a second position, above TP and below CP, where
focus (or topic) may also end up. This projection, which I call αP, recalls
the analysis of Finnish by Holmberg and Nikanne (2002), of Hungarian
by É. Kiss (1995), and of Romance by Uriagereka (1995). These authors
propose that this position is a topic position (see also Saito 2006); and as
we will see, in Japanese, it can host a topic, but it can also host a focused
element under certain circumstances. Because of this flexibility, I propose
calling this projection simply αP as opposed to TopicP or FocusP. In
extending the "EPP" approach to scrambling (e.g., Kitahara 2002, Miyagawa 2001, 2003), Saito (2006) proposes this higher position for Japanese,
arguing that it is a topic position. In section 3.3, I will look in detail at
Saito's proposal and incorporate its core idea into my analysis.

A *mo* expression carries focus stress, indicating that it is associated with
focus.

(11) a. Taroo-wa HON-o   katta.
        Taro-TOP book-ACC bought
        'Taro bought a book.'
     b. TAROO-*mo* hon-o   katta.
        Taro-also   book-ACC bought
        'Taro also bought a book.'

In (11a), which does not contain a *mo* expression, the sentence has neutral
intonation, with the object DP 'book' receiving default prominence. In
(11b), the stress falls not on the object but on the 'also' expression
Taroo-mo. Hasegawa (1991, 1994) notes that when it occurs with sentential negation, the *mo* phrase is interpreted outside the scope of negation.

(12) a. John-mo ko-nakat-ta.
        John-also come-NEG-PAST
        'John (in addition to someone else) did not come.'

b. John-ga   hon-mo   kaw-anakat-ta.

John-NOM book-also buy-NEG-PAST

'A book is one of the things that John did not buy.'

Example (12a) only has the interpretation that there is at least one person who did not come besides John. It does not mean that someone came, but John didn't come as well, which would be the interpretation if the *mo* phrase were inside the scope of negation. Likewise, (12b) only means that John did not buy at least two things, something and a book; it does not mean that John bought something but not also a book.

Early on, Hasegawa (1991) described this phenomenon as the *positive polarity* property of *mo*. According to Hasegawa, at LF the *mo* phrase must be outside the scope of negation to stay true to its positive polarity property. But this is not always true. As shown in (13), a *mo* phrase can indeed occur inside the scope of negation if the negation is in the higher clause.

(13) Taroo-ga [Hanako-ga   suteeki-mo tabeta to] omotte-i-nai.

Taro-NOM Hanako-NOM steak-also ate   C think-NEG

O-susi-dake-da.

HON-sushi-only-COP

'Taro doesn't think that Hanako also ate steak. Just sushi.'

This example has the interpretation that Hanako ate sushi but not also steak. This shows that *mo* is not necessarily a positive polarity item. More recently, Hasegawa (2005) has revised her analysis of *mo*, arguing that it involves a form of agreement (see also Hasegawa 1994). She suggests that T in Japanese is associated with the EPP and that movement of the *mo* phrase is EPP movement to Spec,TP.[3] The *mo* phrase must raise not at LF but in overt syntax. The *mo* phrase raises above negation, which is between vP and TP (see Laka 1990, Pollock 1989). Tree diagrams (14) and (15) show subject and object *mo* phrases. In both cases, the focus feature begins at C and is inherited by T. I represent just the TP level here.

(14)

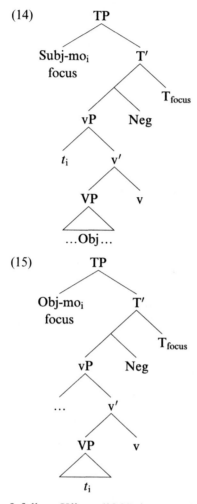

(15)

I follow Klima (1964) in assuming that for an element to occur in the scope of negation, that element must be c-commanded by negation.

We see, then, that the focus on the *mo* phrase is targeted by the focus feature on T. I will give evidence that the *mo* phrase in fact moves to Spec,TP. One immediate observation that gives credence to this claim is that this movement does not allow reconstruction. If it did, we would expect the *mo* phrase to be interpretable inside the scope of sentential negation, something we have already seen is impossible. Lack of reconstruction is a common property of A-movement (see, e.g., Chomsky 1993, Fox 1999, Lasnik 1999a, Miyagawa and Arikawa 2007), and although there is debate about whether all instances of A-movement disallow reconstruction, the fact that the movement of *mo* does not allow reconstruction is a safe indication that it has undergone A-movement. It is an accepted fact that movement to Spec,TP is A-movement, which provides another indication that *mo* moves to Spec,TP, and this movement is triggered by the grammatical feature of focus on T.[4]

The picture that emerges is the following. In languages that have φ-feature agreement, it is typically the case that the goal of the φ-feature agreement is targeted by the agreement on T (or the EPP requirement on T in the traditional approach) and raised to Spec,TP. If there is an external argument, it is this external argument that functions as the goal of φ-feature agreement, and this goal is raised to Spec,TP. We thus have the following observation, repeated from (10).

(16) *A-movement*
   A grammatical feature on T targets the goal of the agreement for movement.

As our discussion of focus in Japanese showed, focus functions in this language exactly the same way that φ-feature agreement does in agreement languages. This, then, is a case where focus functions as a grammatical feature, an idea found in numerous works on focus (e.g., Brody 1990, Horvath 1981, 1986, 1995, É. Kiss 1995). Although some linguists argue that the focus feature is in the CP domain (see, e.g., Culicover and Rochemont 1983), I assume that, just like φ-features in agreement languages, this focus is inherited by T in the cases we observed in Japanese. In a related point, Horvath (1995) argues that in Hungarian, the focus feature appears on T.

If the movement of *mo* raises it to Spec,TP, it is A-movement, not Ā-movement. I will give two arguments that the *mo* phrase undergoes overt A-movement. First, as already noted, A-movement scrambling may overcome a WCO violation (Mahajan 1990, Saito 1992, Tada 1993, Yoshimura 1989). Consider (17). Example (17a) is a typical WCO violation, and (17b) is a typical case of WCO suppression by A-scrambling.

(17) a. ?*[Sakihodo e_i e_j yonda hito$_i$]-ga   futatu-izyou-no
      [just.now   read   person]-NOM two-more.than-GEN
      meiwaku meeru$_j$-o kesita.
      spam   mail-ACC deleted
      'The person who read them just now deleted more than two pieces of spam mail.'

b. Futatu-izyou-no   meiwaku meeru$_j$-o [sakihodo e_i e_j yonda
two-more.than-GEN spam   mail-ACC [just.now   read
hito$_i$]-ga t_j kesita.
person]-NOM   deleted
Lit. 'More than two pieces of spam mail, the person who read
them just now deleted.'

Now note that the WCO violation is suppressed even if the fronted phrase
contains *mo*.

(18) Futatu-izyou-no   meiwaku meeru$_j$-*mo* [sakihodo e_i e_j yonda
two-more.than-GEN spam   mail-also [just.now   read
hito$_i$]-ga t_j kesita.
person]-NOM   deleted
Lit. 'More than two pieces of spam mail also, the person who read
them just now deleted.'

This example demonstrates that the *mo* phrase has undergone A-
movement. We can also see that a *mo* phrase, when locally scrambled,
may function as a new binder for the reciprocal 'each other'.

(19) a. Taroo-to Hanako-o$_i$ otagai-no   sensei-ga t_i
Taro-and Hanako-ACC each.other-GEN teacher-NOM
suisensita.
recommended
'Taro and Hanako, each other's teachers recommended.'
b. Taroo-to Hanako-mo$_i$ otagai-no   sensei-ga t_i
Taro-and Hanako-also each.other-GEN teacher-NOM
suisensita.
recommended
Lit. 'Taro and Hanako also, each other's teachers
recommended.'

We thus have converging evidence that local movement of the *mo* phrase
is A-movement. I will assume that this movement raises *mo* to Spec,TP
(Miyagawa 2005b, 2007; see also Hasegawa 2005), although I will show
that Spec,TP is not the only landing site for A-movement.

A consequence of this analysis is that it predicts that any XP to the left
of the *mo* phrase must have moved there by scrambling. This is shown in
(20), where, according to the proposed analysis, the subject has undergone scrambling to the left of the *mo* object phrase.

(20) John-ga   [TP hon-*mo*   [vP *t*Subj [vP *t*Obj kaw-anaka-]] ta]
     John-NOM   book-also   buy-NEG-PAST

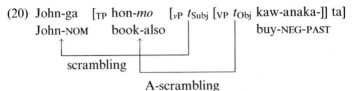

                          scrambling

                             A-scrambling
             'A book is one of the things John did not buy.'

Saito (1985) argues that subjects do not scramble. However, Ko (2007) argues that the subject can, in fact, scramble in Japanese and Korean. If the analysis outlined here is correct, it supports Ko's proposal. Miyagawa and Arikawa (2007) provide further evidence for subject scrambling in Japanese based on the distribution of floating numeral quantifiers.

   In fact, we can use an example similar to the ones in Miyagawa and Arikawa 2007 as evidence for the analysis given above. In the standard analysis of floating numeral quantifiers, a subject separated from its floating quantifier by the object is typically unacceptable (Haig 1980, Kuroda 1980; see Miyagawa and Arikawa 2007 for further discussion).

(21) *Gakusei-ga uisukii-o   futa-ri nonda.
      student-NOM whiskey-ACC two-CL drank
      'Two students drank whiskey.'

The subject floating numeral quantifier is inside the VP, where it cannot be construed with the subject. Now note the following example:

(22) ?Gakusei-ga uisukii-*mo*   futa-ri nonda.
      student-NOM whiskey-also two-CL drank
      'Two students also drank whiskey.'

Although not perfect, this sentence with object *mo* shows marked improvement over (20), at least for those speakers who accept this kind of "nonstandard" case (see Miyagawa and Arikawa 2007 for discussion of the nonstandard cases, which are typically judged to be essentially grammatical as reported in the literature). This is an indication that the object has moved to its left and that the subject, too, has moved to the left of the object. Miyagawa and Arikawa present an analysis in which the object in these nonstandard cases of floating numeral quantifiers occupies Spec,TP, and the subject to its left has undergone Ā-movement. As Miyagawa and Arikawa note, even the "ungrammatical" (21) can be made to sound better with a pause between the object and the subject numeral quantifier, indicating that "double" scrambling is possible even if the subject is not marked by *mo*, which is what we expect.

I will depart from Miyagawa and Arikawa 2007 in one respect. Note that, if Miyagawa and Arikawa are correct that the position to which the subject scrambles in these cases is an Ā-position, we would expect a WCO violation, and we also would not expect the subject to be able to function as a binder (see Hoji and Ishii 2004, Miyamoto and Sugimura 2005). As it turns out, neither of these predictions holds.

(23) Dare$_i$-ga [mukasi   pro$_i$ pro$_j$ hihansita hito$_j$]-mo   t$_j$
     who-NOM long.time.ago   criticized person-also
     sukininatta no?
     came.to.like Q
     Lit. 'Who, the person who (he) criticized a long time ago also came to like?'

(24) Hanako$_i$-ga   zibun-zisin$_i$-mo t$_i$ hihansita.
     Hanako-NOM self-also   criticized
     'Hanako also criticized herself.'

As we can see, the scrambled subject suppresses a WCO violation, and it can create a new binder, both pointing to the fact that this subject is in an A-position. Miyamoto and Sugimura (2005), in criticizing an earlier version of Miyagawa and Arikawa 2007, argue that the scrambled subject is not in an Ā-position but rather in the major subject position (a major subject being an "additional" subject marked by the nominative that appears higher in the structure than the normal subject; see Kuno 1973). Contrary to Miyamoto and Sugimura's proposal, however, the A-position above Spec,TP is not the major subject position, as the following examples show:

(25) a. *[e$_i$ e$_i$ sukizya-nai hito$_j$]-mo   dare$_j$-ni atta no?
            like-not   person-also who-DAT met Q
            Lit. 'The person who doesn't like (him) met who?'
     b. Dare$_j$-ni [e$_i$ e$_i$ sukizya-nai hito$_j$]-mo   t$_j$ atta no?
        who-DAT   like-not   person-also   met Q
        Lit. 'Who, the person who doesn't like (him) met?'

Here, what occurs in the higher A-position is a dative phrase. Because there is no such a thing as a "major dative," the higher A-position must be something other than the major subject position.[5]

3.2.2 αP
The evidence clearly points to the existence of an A-position above TP and below CP. I will adopt a version of a proposal by Saito (2006), who

suggests such a projection. He calls it the "Theme" projection, where *theme* refers to what I am calling *topic*. I will use the more common term *topic*, with the understanding that as I am using it, the term does not necessarily refer to a discourse topic; rather, the topic can simply be the "topic" of the sentence—part of a categorical expression as opposed to a thetic expression in Kuroda's (1972–1973) terms. This way of using *topic* is consonant with Saito's usage of *theme*. In the examples above, the phrase at the head of the sentence, and to the left of the *mo* phrase, is most naturally understood as the topic of the sentence. However, I will revise Saito's proposal and suggest that there is simply a projection, αP, that at times serves to host a topic but at other times may host a focused element. In chapter 4, we will see that α may even host φ-feature agreement in some languages. This αP occurs *as needed*, and if it does occur, the head α hosts the syntactic feature of topic/focus that it inherits from C, making Spec,αP an A-position. If the clause contains just one focus or topic, αP need not occur, and if it does not, the topic/focus feature is inherited by T. There may also be more than one αP, again, if needed. The structure of Japanese when there are two relevant elements—topic and focus, for example—is as shown in (26).

(26)

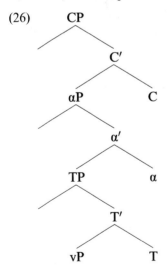

The idea that there is a projection between TP and CP is certainly not novel. For example, in Kikuyu, a Bantu language, this is the position where focused elements occur (Horvath 1995:41); and it is the position that hosts a topic in Finnish (Holmberg and Nikanne 2002) and in Romance (Uriagereka 1995).

For the examples with the *mo* phrase in Spec,TP and the topic in the higher position, I suggest the structure in (27).

(27)

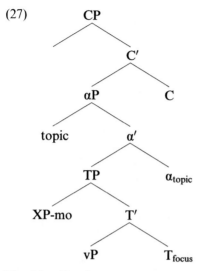

The identification of α with topic is, in this instance, an adoption of Saito's (2006) proposal. However, as we will see, α may host a focused phrase. I have assumed that focus is a syntactic feature, as proposed by Horvath (1981, 1986) and further developed by Brody (1990). I also take from Horvath's work the idea that the focus feature may be assigned to different heads, an idea that departs from Brody 1990 and much other research that assumes a special focus head. I will propose that the focus feature—or, more precisely, a probe that turns into the focus feature, as I will show later—always merges initially on C, and it can stay there, or it can be inherited by a lower head, T (or α if α occurs). What gets passed down to T (or α) forms a parameter that I wish to exploit to unify all A-movements—the "EPP" movement and A-scrambling. One question is, what makes T and α a target for A-movement in a way that C is not? I attempt to answer this question in chapter 4 when I discuss A- and Ā-movements. In what follows, I will give further evidence for the structure in (27).

3.2.3 Nominative Object

Many stative transitive predicates in Japanese allow the object to be marked with nominative instead of accusative case.

(28) Taroo-ga eigo-o/-ga   hanas-e-ru.
     Taro-NOM English-ACC/-NOM speak-can-PRES
     'Taro can speak English.'

It has been observed that the choice of case marking on the object leads
to a difference in scope (Sano 1985, Tada 1992; see also Koizumi 1995,
2008).

(29) a. Kiyomi-wa migime-dake-o   tumur-e-ru.
        Kiyomi-TOP right.eye-only-ACC close-can-PRES
        Lit. 'Kiyomi can just close his right eye.'
        [can > only] 'Kiyomi can wink his right eye.'
     b. Kiyomi-wa migime-dake-ga   tumur-e-ru.
        Kiyomi-TOP right.eye-only-NOM close-can-PRES
        [only > can] 'It is only the right eye that Kiyomi can close.'

In (29a), the accusative object is interpreted below the verb 'can close', so
this sentence means that Kiyomi has the ability to just close his right eye,
thus the translation 'wink'. In contrast, the nominative object in (29b) has
the opposite scope, where the object is interpreted higher than the verb,
which gives the meaning that Kiyomi can only close his right eye. Tada
(1993) and Koizumi (1995) relate the wide scope reading of the nominative object to Case: the nominative Case on the object must raise to a position high in the structure, possibly to the region of T, where it can be
licensed. But this would be an instance of forced movement strictly due
to Case, something that should not occur, as we saw in chapter 1. A point
not noted before is that the nominative object, as opposed to the accusative, tends to be focused, and this focus is further enhanced in these examples by the occurrence of -*dake* 'only'. Given what we have already seen,
the nominative object with focus and the nominative subject, presumably
as topic, both undergo A-movement (Miyagawa 2001), the trigger being
the grammatical features of focus and topic, respectively. This is shown in
the tree diagram in (30).

(30)

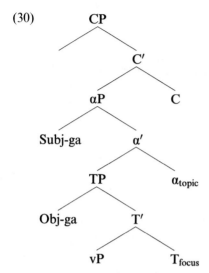

This analysis makes a clear prediction that distinguishes it from earlier Case-based analyses: namely, that if the context allows for defocusing of the nominative object, it should be possible to interpret it in its original object position. Indeed, Nomura (2005) presents examples of precisely this nature (see also Koizumi 2008). Thus, we can assume that the wide scope interpretation of the nominative is focus-related and not due to Case.

When the nominative object does raise, it moves into an A-position—Spec, TP, I assume—because it does not reconstruct. What about the subject? It, too, occupies an A-position, as shown in (31) by the fact that it can bind an anaphor.

(31) Taroo$_i$-ga zibun-zisin$_i$-no sensei-ga   hihan-deki-nakat-ta.
      Taro-NOM self-GEN   teacher-NOM criticize-can-NEG-PAST
      'Taro was unable to criticize his own teacher.'

The relevant portion of the structure for (31) is as follows.

(32) [$_{CP}$[$_{\alpha P}$ Taroo-ga$_i$ [$_{TP}$ zibun-zisin$_i$-no sensei-ga
      Taro-NOM   self-GEN   teacher-NOM
      [$_{vP}$ t_i ... t_j ...] T$_{focus}$] α_{topic}] C]

Later I will give an explanation of how focus and topic emerge.

3.3   Topic Movement

3.3.1   Scrambling as Topicalization

I now turn to the other discourse-configurational feature—topic. As mentioned earlier, *topic* as I am using it refers to the element, usually at the left edge, that represents what the sentence is about. It can be the discourse topic, but it need not be. Japanese has a discourse topic marker *wa*, which typically occurs on a phrase at the left edge of the sentence.

(33) Taroo-*wa* piza-o   tabeta.
     Taro-TOP pizza-ACC ate
     'As for Taro, he ate pizza.'

The *wa* phrase is outside TP, in the CP region (Kuno 1973, Kuroda 1965; see Kishimoto 2006 for evidence that the *wa* phrase is in the CP domain). *Wa* marks the discourse topic, but the construction I am concerned with involves scrambling of a phrase to the left edge of a sentence, as in (34).

(34) Piza-o$_i$ Taroo-ga t_i tabeta.
     pizza-ACC Taro-NOM   ate
     'Pizza, Taro ate.'

I will argue that one instance of this local scrambling is due to the topic feature on the head whose specifier is occupied by 'pizza'.

To get started, let us review the evidence from earlier studies for the proposal that A-scrambling is triggered by an independent EPP feature on T. Since we now assume that there is no independent EPP feature, but that instead, movement is triggered in conjunction with some grammatical feature, we need to search for what we can take from the earlier "EPP" analysis and what parts of that analysis we can set aside. I will first present the argument for the earlier analysis, then point out some problems, and finally propose a new analysis based on "topic" (and "focus") as a feature that triggers this "EPP" movement, adopting an idea suggested by Saito (2006).

The test given in Miyagawa 2001 (see also Miyagawa 2003) to argue for the "EPP" basis of A-scrambling involves the Japanese universal quantifier *zen'in* 'all' and its interpretation relative to sentential negation. As shown in (35), *zen'in* 'all' in object position may have the partial negation interpretation of 'not all'. (The other reading, 'all > not', is probably due to a collective reading of 'all'.)

(35) Taroo-ga *zen'in-o* sikar-anakat-ta.
     Taro-NOM all-ACC scold-NEG-PAST
     'Taro didn't scold all.'
     not > all (all > not)

As noted by Kato (1988), when a universal expression is in subject position, it is interpreted outside the scope of negation (with neutral intonation).

(36) *Zen'in-ga* siken-o uke-nakat-ta.
　　　all-NOM   test-ACC take-NEG-PAST
　　　'All did not take the test.'
　　　*not > all, all > not

In contrast, as noted in Miyagawa 2001, if the object is scrambled, the subject universal expression may be interpreted inside the scope of negation.

(37) Siken-o$_i$ *zen'in-ga* t_i uke-nakat-ta.
　　　test-ACC all-NOM   take-NEG-PAST
　　　'All didn't take the test.'
　　　not > all, all > not

Thus, when 'all' is in subject position in the SOV order, as in (36), the preferred reading is 'all > not'. When the object is scrambled to the left edge, as in (37), partial negation becomes possible.

　　How does negation take scope over 'all' to achieve the partial negation interpretation? In (36), where the subject 'all' is outside the scope of negation, 'all' begins in Spec,vP and moves to a position outside the c-command domain of negation. A reasonable assumption is that it moves to Spec,TP as shown in (38). (The position of negation in (38) is roughly as proposed by Laka (1990) and Pollock (1989).)

(38)

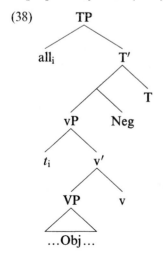

In (38), where the subject 'all' occurs in the scrambled order OSV, it is able to be interpreted inside the scope of negation. The simplest assumption to make here is that this subject 'all' stays in situ in Spec,vP, a situation made possible by the movement of the object to Spec,TP.

(39)

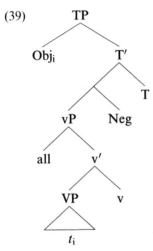

These structures suggest that something—subject, object—raises to Spec,TP, even though the raised XP is not focused, or need not be (Miyagawa 2001; see also Miyagawa 2003). If the subject moves to Spec,TP, the object stays in situ, as in (38). On the other hand, if the object moves to Spec,TP, this allows the subject to stay in situ, as shown in (39).[6] Although in (39) I only represent the movement from inside VP to Spec,TP, if we are to follow the requirements imposed by the notion of phases, the object must first move and adjoin to vP, a point I will return to at the end of this chapter. Finally, the OSV order with the universal in subject position has another interpretation in which the subject takes wide scope over negation. This results from a derivation in which the subject first moves to Spec,TP and the object then moves to a higher position. I will return to both of these derivations later.

3.3.2 The Kumamoto Dialect of Japanese

There is dramatic evidence from a recent study of the Kumamoto dialect of Japanese by Kato (2007) for the type of "EPP" analysis I gave above. Unlike standard Japanese, this dialect, which is spoken on the southern island of Kyushu, distinguishes between two types of nominative case marking.

(40) *Nominative marking*
   Standard Japanese: ga
   Kumamoto: ga, no
   (Yoshimura 1994)

According to Kato (2007), the two kinds of nominative marking occur in different syntactic environments. *Ga* occurs as the nominative marker outside vP, and *no* as the nominative marker inside vP. We can see this in multiple-nominative constructions like (41), from Yoshimura 1994:20.

(41) Kumamoto-*ga*   baniku-*no*   umaka.
   Kumamoto-NOM horse.meat-NO tasty
   'It is Kumamoto where horse meat tastes good.'

However, in a normal transitive construction, in the SOV order the subject must have *ga*.[7]

(42) a.   Taroo-ga sakana-ba tabeta-bai.
        Taro-NOM fish-ACC   ate-FINAL.PARTICLE
        'Taro ate fish.'
   b. ?*Taroo-no sakana-ba tabeta-bai.
        Taro-NO fish-ACC   ate-FINAL.PARTICLE

This is consistent if we assume that the subject in (42a) necessarily undergoes "EPP" movement to Spec,TP, where it is outside vP, hence must be marked by *ga*. Kato (2007:122) further notes the following crucial example:

(43) Sakana-ba Taroo-no tabeta-bai.
   fish-ACC   Taro-NO ate-FINAL.PARTICLE

Here, the object has scrambled to the head of the sentence. Crucially, now it is possible for the subject to be marked with the "vP" nominative *no*. This indicates that because of the scrambling of the object, the subject may stay in situ in Spec,vP. This, again, shows that if something occurs in Spec,TP, everything else, including the subject, may stay in situ—a typical EPP effect. Finally, Kato notes that in a variant of (43), the subject may be marked with *ga* as well.

(44) Sakana-ba Taroo-ga tabeta-bai.
   fish-ACC   Taro-NOM ate-FINAL.PARTICLE

This is the derivation in which the subject first moves to Spec,TP, so that it receives the nominative marking *ga*. The object then undergoes movement to a position above this Spec,TP.

Finally, recall that the focus phrase *mo* moves to Spec,TP.

(45) a. Taroo-mo hon-o   katta.
Taro-also book-ACC bought
'Taro also bought a book.'
b. Taroo-ga hon-mo   katta.
Taro-NOM book-also bought
'Taro bought a book, too.'

Earlier, I gave evidence based on Hasegawa's (2005) analysis that the *mo* phrase in both of these examples moves to Spec,TP overtly. This proposal in turn predicts that, if the *mo* object phrase in (45b) scrambles to the left of the subject, it moves to Spec,TP. This prediction is confirmed by the Kumamoto dialect (thanks to Sachiko Kato for providing the examples).

(46) a. Inu-ga   booru-mo kuwaetekita.
dog-NOM ball-also   chewed
'The dog also chewed a ball.'
b. Booru-mo inu-no kuwaetekita.
ball-also   dog-NO chewed
'The ball, the dog also chewed.'

As shown in (46b), scrambling the *mo* phrase makes it possible for the subject 'dog' to be marked by *no*. It can also be marked by *ga*, but the important point is that *no* is possible.

3.3.3   A Problem with the EPP Analysis

The EPP analysis of A-scrambling is couched in the earlier notion of the EPP—that every T is associated with the EPP property (Alexiadou and Anagnostopoulou 1998, Chomsky 1981, 1995). However, as we saw in chapter 1, this is simply false; so-called EPP movement only emerges when some relevant grammatical feature is present, typically φ-feature agreement (e.g., Chomsky 2000, 2001, 2005, Kuroda 1988, Miyagawa 2005b). If it is true that in languages such as Japanese, topic/focus constitutes a grammatical feature equivalent to φ-feature agreement, we would expect "EPP" movement to occur only in the presence of topic/focus, not every time the structure contains a T. In other words, there is no such thing as "EPP" independent of relevant grammatical features (Miyagawa 2005b).

Indeed, a problem with applying the traditional EPP to scrambling is noted in Miyagawa 2001. There, I point out that, contrary to Kato's (1988) observation, the universal quantifier in subject position even in

SOV order can take scope inside negation when put in an embedded context. The following example, taken from Saito 2006, demonstrates the same point:

(47) Zen'in-ga siken-o   erab-ana-i   to omou.
     all-NOM   exam-ACC choose-NEG-PRES C think
     'I think that all will not choose an exam (over a term paper).'
     all > not, not > all

Saito concludes that the "EPP" effects observed in Miyagawa 2001, 2003 are what he calls "interpretational" effects that commonly appear in root clauses. In his approach, this is a left-edge effect of cartography as studied by Rizzi (1997, 2004) and others. I have already shown that focus triggers movement in Japanese to Spec,TP. I will extend this idea and adopt Saito's proposal that the EPP movement identified in Miyagawa 2001, 2003 and other works is a function of "topic," thereby unifying movement in Japanese under what É. Kiss (1995) has called discourse configurationality. Thus, movement of the subject or the object, or even some other element, in A-scrambling is a form of movement triggered by a grammatical feature, which in Japanese happens to be either topic or focus, given that Japanese is a discourse-configurational language. If such a feature occurs, as it usually does in the root clause, it results in the type of EPP effects we saw earlier. Thus, in SOV or OSV word order, the leftmost element (S or O) has undergone movement due to a grammatical feature with an "interpretational" effect, most likely "topic" in a broad sense, although focus might play a role in certain cases. In the subordinate clause, such an interpretational effect typically does not arise because topic is less apt to appear in such a context. The situation would be different if focus were present, of course.

On this discourse-configurational view, the phrases on the left edge in (36) and (37), repeated here, carry some information-structural meaning.

(48) *Zen'in-ga* siken-o uke-nakat-ta.
     all-NOM   test-ACC take-NEG-PAST
     'All did not take the test.'

(49) Siken-o$_i$ *zen'in-ga* t_i uke-nakat-ta.
     test-ACC all-NOM   take-NEG-PAST
     'All didn't take the test.'
     not > all, all > not

The subject 'all' in (48) and the scrambled object 'test' in (49) are both topics—they both represent what the sentence is about. It is possible with an identificational ("narrow") focus intonation that 'all' in (48) could alternatively be interpreted as focus, but I will keep to the neutral intonation. The question is, where is this "topic" in (48) and (49)?

Let us look at Saito's (2006) analysis of these sentences. Saito proposes that there is a projection above TP, which he calls ThP (ThemeP). (This is where I postulate instead the category αP.) In essence, his analysis captures at this Theme level what I earlier suggested for the TP level (Miyagawa 2001, 2003): either the subject or the object may occupy Spec,ThP, allowing the other—object or subject—to stay inside the scope of negation. The structure Saito suggests for (48), where 'all' in the SOV order takes scope over sentential negation, is shown in (50).

(50)

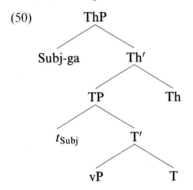

That is, the subject first moves to Spec,TP, apparently because of the EPP requirement on T (see Saito's example (25)). It then moves to Spec,ThP and gets interpreted as the topic of the sentence. An argument Saito gives to explain why 'all' has to move to Spec,ThP to escape the scope of negation has to do with the fact that in English, a universal quantifier in Spec,TP is known to be able to take scope inside negation.

(51) Everyone had not left the party. There were still people talking and drinking.

As Saito suggests, topic is a left-edge effect, and it does not, or need not, occur in subordinate structures. This explains the fact observed in Miyagawa 2001 that in subordinate clauses, the universal in subject position may take scope inside negation even in SOV order. I will adopt Saito's idea that topic does not, or need not, occur in subordinate structures precisely for the reason he gives, that it is a left-edge effect. However, I will depart from his analysis in not identifying topic with a particular projection. Rather, I will suggest that topic as I am using the term may occur on one head or another—T or α—depending on other factors in the structure.

Although the fact illustrated in (51) is all that Saito notes about English, there is, in fact, evidence that something comparable to ThP exists even in English. On the basis of comparing English with Italian and French, Belletti (1990) suggests that a subject that precedes a sentential adverb, or something akin to it, is in a topicalized position (in Belletti's framework, this means an adjunction position, but that does not concern us here).

(52) John probably/unfortunately has already talked to Mary.

In a related point, in Miyagawa 1993, I gave evidence that the universal quantifier in subject position in English cannot take scope inside negation if it is separated from the rest of the sentence (*Everyone has been not turning in their papers*). A more appropriate example for the issue at hand is this:

(53) Everyone probably/unfortunately/as far as I know has not done the homework.

Here it is difficult, if not impossible, to interpret the universal inside the scope of negation. This, then, is empirical evidence for Saito's suggestion that at least in English, the universal in Spec,TP can be in the scope of sentential negation. But does the same hold in Japanese? I will return to this question after completing the description of Saito's proposal. For the scrambled order in (49), in which the object has moved to sentence-initial position across the subject, Saito proposes that the initial scrambling is adjunction to TP (see also Saito 1985).

(54)

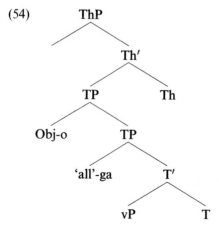

Saito suggests two possible derivations besides (54). In one option, the object moves to Spec,ThP, and the subject 'all' stays in Spec,TP and gets interpreted inside the scope of negation. If, however, the object does not move to Spec,ThP, it reconstructs at LF to its original object position. This opens the way for the subject 'all' to move to Spec,ThP at LF, giving the other possible reading where 'all' takes scope over negation.

Saito assumes that Spec,TP is within the scope of negation, basing his assumption on the English example in (51) (*Everyone had not left the party...*). There is a second way to view the lack of reconstruction in English and Japanese. In both languages, topic movement (and presumably also focus movement) to Spec,TP or Spec,αP does not reconstruct. In English, the topic may move only to αP, since Spec,TP is reserved for ϕ-feature agreement, but in Japanese, the topic may move either to Spec,TP or to Spec,αP. I will assume this alternative view of "lack of reconstruction." As one piece of evidence, recall that in the double-nominative construction, the second nominative, which is the object, is normally focused and occupies Spec,TP. As noted earlier, the nominative object is typically interpreted high in the structure; thus, it does not reconstruct if moved to Spec,TP. Sentence (55) provides another example of this (Miyagawa 2001).

(55) Taroo-ga zen'in-ga home-rare-nakat-ta.
     Taro-NOM all-NOM   praise-can-NEG-PAST
     'Taro was not able to praise all.'
     all > not, *not > all

The nominative object in Spec,TP takes scope outside of negation. To ensure that we are dealing with the relevant structure, we need to verify that the nominative object is in Spec,TP and the nominative subject is in the A-position above it. Example (56) gives evidence for this.

(56) Taroo-to Hanako$_i$-ga [otagai$_i$-no   zen'in-no sensei]-ga
     Taro-and Hanako-NOM each.other-GEN all-GEN   teachers-NOM
     home-rare-nakat-ta.
     praise-can-NEG-PAST
     'Taro and Hanako could not praise every one of each other's teachers.'

It is possible to interpret the nominative object outside the scope of negation, which, after all, is the more natural interpretation, and at the same time understand the reciprocal to refer to 'Taro and Hanako', indicating that 'Taro and Hanako' is in an A-position—that is, in Spec,αP.

Saito suggests that in the OSV order, the nominative subject moves to Spec,TP because of the EPP feature on T (Saito's example (30)). However, with the "agreement" approach to the EPP that I am assuming, unless the subject is focused or is a topic, there is no reason for it to move to Spec,TP; the EPP effect only arises if some relevant grammatical feature is present. I will assume that if a sentence contains just one topic, and no focus, its structure has no αP (Saito's ThP) and the topic feature occurs directly on T, having been inherited from C (a point I take up below). Tree (57) illustrates this configuration.

(57)

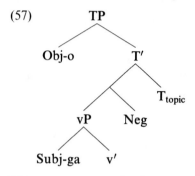

This structure contains just one grammatical feature, topic, and it raises the object to Spec,TP. (Later I will argue that topic and focus are the same feature, differentiated essentially by the context in which they occur.) The subject stays in situ in Spec,vP, where it can be interpreted inside the scope of negation. In the other possible scope situation with the same OSV word order, in which the subject takes scope outside negation, the subject is raised to Spec,TP either as topic or as focus. The object may be raised to αP, an instance of A-movement, or to a higher position, possibly Spec,CP—an Ā-position.

Finally, if a sentence contains two elements—some combination of topic and/or focus—αP is projected. We expect that Spec,αP can host a focused phrase as well as a topic. Sentence (58) illustrates this situation: it contains a *mo* phrase followed by a scrambled phrase that can antecede an anaphor. This scrambled phrase is not associated with focus in the default intonation; hence, we can assume that it is a topic.

(58) John-ni-mo$_i$ Taroo-to Hanako-o$_j$ [otagai$_i$-no   tomodati]-ga
     John-DAT-also Taro-and Hanako-ACC each.other-GEN friends-NOM
     t_i t_j syookaisita.
          introduced

Lit. 'To John also, Taro and Hanako, each other's friends introduced.'

(59) [$_{aP=focus}$ John-ni-mo   [$_{TP=topic}$ Taroo-to Hanako-o
        John-DAT-also   Taro-and Hanako-ACC
      [$_{vP}$ ...] T$_{topic}$] α_{focus}]

Next, I will discuss the feature relevant to topic and focus movement.[8]

3.4 Assigning Topic and Focus

In this section, I will develop an analysis of topic and focus consistent with the idea that they are computationally equivalent to ϕ-feature agreement. When inherited by T (or in certain circumstances, α), either of these features triggers A-movement. The idea that topic and focus play a syntactic role in some languages is not new. In her work on discourse configurationality, É. Kiss identifies these two as being expressed in the syntax of languages such as Hungarian (É. Kiss 1995, 1997, 2003). In the cartographic approach to linguistic structure (e.g., Rizzi 1997, 2004), topic and focus are part of the articulated CP system. The topic and focus that we have been discussing start at C, and in the Japanese-type languages they are inherited by T. This picture differs from most treatments of topic and focus in the literature. In É. Kiss's and Rizzi's work, topic and focus typically are each associated with a special head with the relevant property, Topic or Focus (on the latter, see also Brody 1990). There are exceptions to this treatment of topic and focus as being associated with topic and focus heads. One is Maki, Kaiser, and Ochi's (1999) proposal that the topic feature begins at T and raises to C. Another is Horvath's (1995) argument that focus in Hungarian occurs as a grammatical feature on T, and not on a special focus head.

A number of questions arise when we view topic and focus as syntactic features. First, what precisely is the feature for each? Second, why is it that one feature does not interfere with the other? If they did, we would expect either that only one of them could show up within a given clause, or that the two would be in a highly restrictive ordering relation. Neither is the case: topic and focus can both occur in the same clause, and the ordering of phrases associated with each appears to be free both before and after movement (they do need to be in the local domain for A-movement). An obvious answer is that topic and focus are two distinct features, inherently already valued as such, and because of this, they do not interfere with each other. That seems reasonable, and much of the literature on the issue assumes this. However, by simply separating topic and focus, we are potentially missing some important insights. As a prelude to showing this, I will briefly discuss Holmberg and Nikanne's (2002) proposal about the notion of topic, which I will adopt and extend.

Finnish has a topic position above TP and below CP. The following examples are from Holmberg and Nikanne (H&N) 2002:78:

(60) a. Graham Greene on kirjoittanut tämän kirjan.
        Graham Greene has written   this   book
        'Graham Greene has written this book.'
     b. Tämän kirjan on kirjoittanut Graham Greene.
        this   book has written   Graham Greene

The two examples mean essentially the same, although, as H&N note, (60b) most naturally translates into a passive sentence in English (*This book was written by Graham Greene*). H&N propose that in both examples, the phrase at the head of the sentence ('Graham Greene' in (60a), 'this book' in (60b)) occurs in the topic position, which they label as *FP* for *Finite P*, a term taken from cartography. To avoid confusion with *F(ocus)P*, I will use the label *FinP* instead.

(61) a. [$_{CP}$[$_{FinP}$ Graham Greene [$_{TP}$ ... this book ...]]]
     b. [$_{CP}$[$_{FinP}$ this book [$_{TP}$ ... Graham Greene ...]]]

H&N assume that the topic moves to Spec,FinP through the typical process of agreement, and for this, they postulate the feature −focus as the feature for topic, which they assign to the Fin head. This −focus on the Fin head is comparable to the probe. Moreover, they postulate that the same −focus is automatically assigned to every phrase in the string, unless a phrase has the +focus feature to begin with. The "probe" −focus on Fin picks out one of these −focus phrases and raises it to Spec,FinP. The −focus features on the remaining phrases are deleted.

Is topicalization always required in Finnish? With very few exceptions, the −focus feature apparently occurs in every sentence, but even with this feature, topicalization does not take place if the "topic expletive" *sitä* occupies Spec,FinP.

(62) Sitä ovat nämä lapset   jo   oppineet imaan.
     EXPL have these children already learned to.swim
     'These children have already learned to swim.'

As H&N note, and as (62) shows, the expletive is not related to any item in the sentence. It is "a pure expletive.... [I]t has no φ-features and is thus not directly involved in any Case or agreement checking. It is also not a placeholder for the subject. Its function is just to check the EPP feature [of −focus]" (H&N 2002:90). H&N suggest that the expletive *sitä* is associated not with any φ-feature (or Case), but with the "topic" feature −focus, although *sitä* is obviously not a topic. −Focus requires something in its specifier, which is normally the topic, but the expletive may occur instead, preventing topicalization from taking place. From the present perspective, the occurrence of this expletive that is associated with topic is further confirmation that topic (and, by implication, focus) functions as a grammatical feature that triggers movement in some languages. Finnish also has φ-feature agreement—so here is a language that combines both agreement and discourse-configurational properties, a point I return to in chapter 4.

H&N's system leads to two general observations.

(63) Generalizing H&N's approach to Finnish topic, we can say that
    a. topic is default, whereas focus is marked; and
    b. topic is not uniquely associated with any particular phrase in the structure.

Topic is default and focus is marked, in that the −focus feature, which represents topic, is automatically assigned to all phrases. The one exception to this is a phrase that is focused because it already has the +focus feature; +focus is therefore marked. Turning to the second point, there are two ways in which the topic is not associated with any particular phrase in the structure. First, the "probe" −focus on Fin can pick any phrase that has −focus; it just needs to pick one. Essentially, any phrase that isn't marked +focus will do. Second, the "probe" −focus can be satisfied by inserting the "topic expletive" *sitä*, and this expletive is clearly not associated with any associate NP in the structure. It simply fills in the gap to satisfy the feature −focus.

Given these observations, let us make the following assumption:

(64) *Topic/Focus*
    The default feature for topic/focus is −focus (topic).

For the marked property of focus, I propose the following characterization:

(65) *Focus as a marked feature*

   If −focus at C enters into agreement with a focused phrase
   (+focus), −focus is valued as +focus.

That is, the default −focus undergoes valuation as +focus under agreement with a focused phrase. The focused phrase brings the +focus feature
with it from the lexicon, as does the *mo* phrase in Japanese; or the +focus
feature may simply be assigned to it at numeration. Finally, suppose the
following characterization for the idea that −focus at C (the probe) is not
associated with any particular phrase in the structure, which is close to
what H&N propose:

(66) *Topic as free movement*

   The −focus topic feature, once inherited by T or α, simply requires
   its specifier to be filled.

The −focus feature that does not enter into an agreement with a focused
phrase will be inherited by T or α without picking out a goal. The only
thing this −focus requires is that its specifier be filled, as we saw from
the "topic expletive" construction in Finnish. In H&N's terminology,
−focus in Finnish has the "pure" EPP feature. I assume this for all
instances of topic of the type we are dealing with in discourse-
configurational languages. Below, I give some sample derivations to illustrate the default, "pure" EPP nature of topics and the marked nature of
focus.

   The simplest cases are those that contain just one topic or just one
focus. A one-topic sentence has the derivation in (67).

(67) *One-topic sentence*

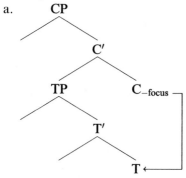

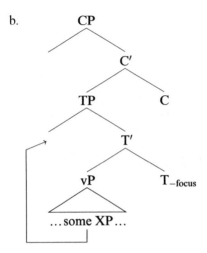

As shown, the −focus feature that does not enter into an agreement (with +focus) is inherited by T from C. This −focus feature on T simply requires that its specifier be filled, which has the effect of marking whatever fills this position as −focus (i.e., as topic). The one exception is the merging of the expletive *sitä* into this position in Finnish; this merger plugs up the topic position, so that the sentence is without a topic.

A one-focus sentence has the derivation in (68).

(68) *One-focus sentence*

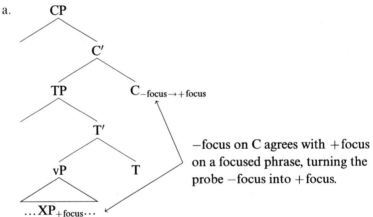

−focus on C agrees with +focus on a focused phrase, turning the probe −focus into +focus.

b.

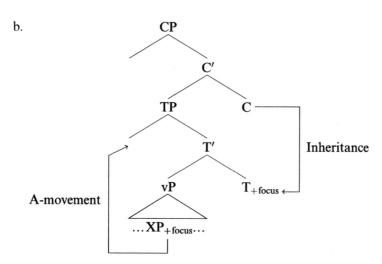

As shown in (68a), if −focus at C enters into agreement with a focused phrase, this −focus is valued as +focus by the goal, thus becoming a marked feature.

What if there are two phrases, one topic and one focus? The proposed analysis predicts that either order should be possible. The reason is that while focus involves a probe-goal relation, topic does not. The derivation for a topic-focus order is illustrated in (69).

(69) *Two phrases: Topic and focus*

a.

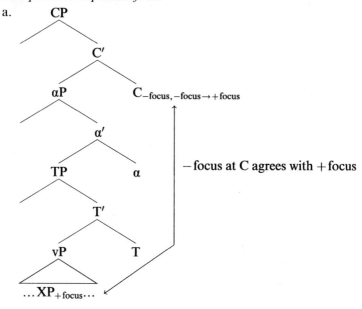

b.

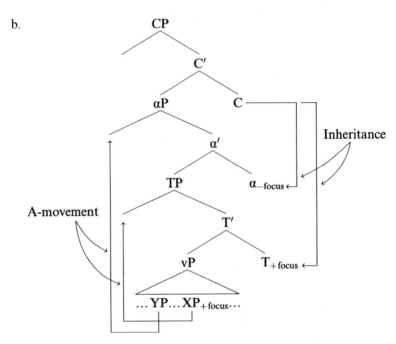

One of the −focus features at C agrees with +focus via agreement, which values the −focus as +focus, and when +focus is inherited by T, the goal comes up to its specifier. The other −focus feature is inherited by α, and the phrase that moves to its specifier is given the attribution of topic. Because there is no probing by the −focus feature, the features do not interfere with each other, and as a result, phrases that end up as topic and focus can occur in either order, both before and after movement. This also holds true for two-topic structures, which are commonly found in Japanese in double-scrambling constructions.

(70) Hanako-ni$_i$ tegami-o$_j$ Taroo-ga t_i t_j okutta.
      Hanako-DAT letter-ACC Taro-NOM   sent
      Lit. 'Hanako, letter, Taro sent.'

Finally, let us look at a two-focus construction. Here, phrases are strictly ordered.

(71) a.   Taroo-mo piza-mo   tabeta.
          Taro-also pizza-also ate
          'Taro also ate pizza, too.'
     b. *Piza-mo   Taroo-mo tabeta.
          pizza-also Taro-also ate

Example (71b) can only have the improbable meaning that a pizza (and something else) ate Taro, too. We can predict this on the assumption made earlier that focus is marked, and that this markedness comes from agreement. The fact that there is agreement means that there is a probe-goal relation, and we would expect two identical features on two different heads (T and α) to be impossible given Locality. This can only mean that there is just one −focus feature that enters into multiple agreement with the two focus phrases. As Richards (2001) notes, when there is one feature that attracts two elements, the closer element (here, the subject *Taroo-mo*) is attracted first, then the lower one (here, *piza-mo*) is tucked in underneath the first, giving rise in this case to the ordering *Taroo-mo − piza-mo*. The other ordering violates Locality as defined by Richards. In contrast, for topics, no such ordering restriction exists. Thus, the scrambled phrases in the double-scrambling example (70) could occur in either order. This is expected because the "topic" −focus feature does not probe.

3.5   Summary

In this chapter, I extended the agreement–topic/focus parameter proposed in chapter 1 and showed how this parameter can characterize A-movements across languages, both A-movement of the typical "EPP" type found in English and other Indo-European languages and the A-scrambling found in many scrambling languages. The idea is that topic/focus is a grammatical feature in discourse-configurational languages that functions in a manner equivalent to φ-feature agreement in agreement languages. When a grammatical feature (topic/focus, φ-feature) is inherited by T, the goal of the grammatical feature raises to T by A-movement. I introduced a projection, αP, above TP and below CP; the α head may also host a grammatical feature, and I showed how, when there are two grammatical features—topic and topic/focus, for example—one occurs on α and the other on T, and both give rise to A-movements.

Finally, I extended Holmberg and Nikanne's (2002) treatment of topic in Finnish, suggesting that "topic" and "focus" arise from the same feature. The default is "topic," as indicated by the feature −focus. If this feature does not enter into agreement with a goal, it occurs as −focus on T (or α). Any given element may undergo free movement to the specifier of T (or α) with −focus, and that element is marked as the topic of the sentence. If −focus enters into agreement with a focused element—that is, an element bearing the feature +focus—it is valued as +focus, and inherited by T or α. This valued +focus feature attracts the focused goal to its specifier. The difference between topic (default) and focus (marked) in turn explains the distribution of these items. Topics occur freely in either order, and a topic can also occur with one focus, again in free order (topic-focus or focus-topic). It is in two-focus structures where we find an ordering restriction: a strict superiority effect arises when one +focus enters into multiple agreement with two focus elements, and the lower focus element must tuck in under the higher one.

I left one question unanswered: why is the head α an "A" head like T and unlike C? I turn to this question in the next chapter.

4 αP, φ-Features, and the A/Ā Distinction

4.1 Introduction

In chapter 3, I proposed αP as a projection that occurs between TP and CP, following similar proposals in the literature (e.g., Holmberg and Nikanne 2002, É. Kiss 1995, Uriagereka 1995).

(1)

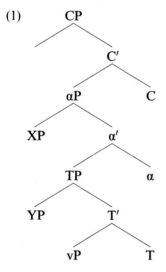

In a language such as Japanese, we saw that αP occurs in the root clause, but need not occur in subordinate clauses.

In this chapter, I explore cases in which α inherits not only topic/focus from C but also the φ-probe, as diagrammed in (2).

(2)

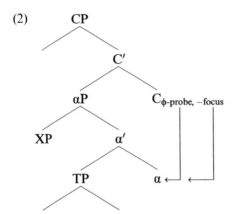

What will a language look like in this situation? First of all, given that the ɸ-probe is incapable of seeking its goal by itself, and α is not a Case assigner, we predict that something other than the ɸ-probe must be inherited on the same head α to allow the ɸ-probe to enter into an Agree relation. In other words, the fact that the ɸ-probe is inherited in tandem with –focus is not coincidental, but necessary. The –focus feature is responsible for locating the goal for the ɸ-feature in the absence of Case. Suppose that –focus itself has not entered into an Agree relation. This means that it requires an XP to raise to its specifier position, where the XP is given the interpretation of topic. It is at this point that the interpretable ɸ-feature on the XP values the ɸ-probe on α. On this view, we predict the following:

(3) The goal of the ɸ-probe at α is the topic of the sentence.

This is in essence the biconditional that Baker (2003) observes for a range of languages including Kinande, a Bantu language that we will look at in detail in this chapter.

(4) A verb X agrees with an NP Y if and only if Y is in a dislocated, adjunct position. (Baker 2003:109)

Dislocated, adjunct position here means a topic position, something I will return to. Baker explains this biconditional by stating that the languages to which it applies lack Case. I will show that Baker is correct that, when the biconditional does apply, it does so because Case is absent. This is so because the ɸ-probe occurs on α and not on T. As I will also show, however, Case effects do show up in certain environments; one cannot say that in these languages Case simply doesn't matter. Where αP is disallowed, the ɸ-probe is inherited by T, and in this environment, we observe the familiar subject-verb agreement, showing the effect of nominative Case.

I begin in section 4.2 by discussing Kinande as analyzed by Baker (2003) and others. I first present Baker's analysis and show that it is consistent with a structure that contains the projection αP. I also introduce new data based on consultation with a native speaker of Kinande that further support my analysis. In section 4.3, I take up Kilega, another Bantu language, basing the discussion on work by Carstens (2005) and Kinyalolo (1991). I look in particular at *wh*-movement, a form of Ā-movement. I then explore ways to distinguish A- and Ā-movements in the kind of approach I am pursuing. I suggest that the phase architecture provides a natural way to distinguish these two types of movement.

4.2 Kinande and αP

For this discussion of Kinande, I depend on the analysis and insights found in Baker 2003 but also draw from Progovac 1993 and Schneider-Zioga 2007.

Kinande has agreement—in fact, quite an elaborate agreement system that allows agreement not only between the subject and the verbal affix but also between the verbal affix and the object or the locative. These possibilities are illustrated in (5) (Baker 2003:113).

(5) a. Omukali mo-a-seny-ire   olukwi (lw'-omo-mbasa).   (SVO)
        woman.1 AFF-1.S/T-chop-EXT wood.11 LK11-LOC.18-axe.9
        'The woman chopped wood (with an axe).'

    b. Olukwi si-lu-li-seny-a   bakali (omo-mbasa).   (OVS)
        wood.11 NEG-11.S-PRES-chop-FV women.2 LOC.18-axe.9
        'Women do not chop wood (with an axe).'

    c. ?Omo-mulongo mw-a-hik-a   omukali.   (LocVS)
        LOC.18-village.3 18.S-T-arrive-FV woman
        'At the village arrived a woman.'

Example (5a) shows the SVO order, and (5b) illustrates the "object reversal" order of OVS. In (5c), the locative phrase occurs in the agreeing position. As in English, this locative inversion occurs in Kinande only with unaccusative and passive verbs, but unlike in English, the locative enters into agreement with the verbal inflection, which suggests that the locative phrase in Kinande is a DP, not a PP.

Along with this three-way option for agreeing (subject, object, locative), Kinande exhibits a property that Baker characterizes as "dislocation." As noted by Baker (2003) and Progovac (1993), the agreeing phrase must be interpreted as definite (or specific). This is illustrated with the object reversal order in (6).

(6) Eritunda, n-a-ri-gul-a.
fruit.5   1SG.S-T-OM5-buy-FV
'The fruit, I bought it.'

In this reversal construction, the object is in a position to trigger agreement on the verbal inflection, and it must be interpreted as definite (i.e., as a topic). This is claimed to be true for all agreeing phrases, a point I will evaluate later. Baker notes that "[t]rue polysynthetic languages... always have agreement and always have dislocation" (2003:112). By *dislocation*, Baker means that he views the agreeing phrase, such as the object in (6), as being somewhere above Spec,TP—he assumes that it is in a higher Spec,TP—in a position comparable to the dislocation position in languages such as Italian. In Romance, dislocation is possible only if the phrase is definite or specific (Rizzi 1986). The agreement, therefore, occurs with a phrase that is in a specifier higher than the normal Spec,TP. Baker expresses this observation as a biconditional for languages such as Kinande (and Mohawk, etc.) and contends that it is a parameter for polysynthetic languages such as Kinande.

(7) A verb X agrees with an NP Y if and only if Y is in a dislocated, adjunct position. (Baker 2003:109)

How is the agreeing phrase "dislocated"? Baker's analysis forces the agreeing phrase to occur in a higher position—thus forces the agreement to hold between this higher specifier and some head—by requiring *pro* to occur in Spec,TP (Baker 2003:124).

(8) $[_{TP}$ NP$_i$ $[_{TP}$ *pro*$_i$ T$\langle$Agr$_i\rangle$+Verb...$[_{VP}$ t_i...$]]]$

The occurrence of *pro* in the lower Spec,TP meets the EPP requirement of T (the assumption here being that there is an independent EPP feature, something that I do not assume); thus, in Kinande the EPP feature is located on T (Baker 2003:125). Moreover, this *pro*, by virtue of occurring in the "normal" Spec,TP, is the actual agreeing phrase; but because it is unpronounced, a fully specified NP that corresponds to the *pro*, NP$_i$, may occur in the higher specifier of TP. If a fully specified DP does not occur, a *pro*-drop construction results, and in Bantu, only the agreeing phrase (subject, object, locative) can be *pro* (Vicki Carstens, pers. comm.).

What forces the *pro* to occur in the lower Spec,TP? According to Baker (2003), the reason is that Kinande has no structural Case. Because no

Case is assigned to the lower Spec,TP (or any other position), no fully specified DP can occur in the lower Spec,TP—yet something must occur in this position to satisfy the EPP requirement on T. Following earlier work (Baker 1996), Baker (2003) suggests that *pro* fits the bill: not requiring Case itself, it can occur in Spec,TP without Case and meet the EPP requirement.

Baker (2003) suggests the following way of comparing Kinande and Romance:

(9) Kinande: agreement, EPP, ~~Case~~
    Romance: agreement, ~~EPP~~, Case

In Kinande, agreement occurs in tandem with the EPP. Because there is no Case, any DP within the local domain of the agreement can become the goal of agreement—the subject, the object, or the locative. Once agreement is established, the DP is raised to Spec,TP to satisfy the EPP. In Romance, Spec,TP is not filled, according to Alexiadou and Anagnostopoulou (1998), and agreement always goes with the subject. Baker describes this state of affairs by claiming that T lacks the EPP requirement in Romance (however that lack is to be accounted for—perhaps along the lines suggested in Alexiadou and Anagnostopoulou 1998). The fact that agreement always goes with the subject in Romance is due to the occurrence of Case—specifically, nominative Case.

The other relevant property of Kinande is that the agreeing phrase must occur on the left edge, where it is interpreted as definite or specific. One piece of evidence for this involves augment vowels (Baker 2003, Progovac 1993, Schneider-Zioga 2007). Nouns in Kinande sometimes begin with an augment vowel that matches the vowel of the class that the noun prefix belongs to. This augment vowel may drop under the scope of negation and in some other contexts. The following sentences exemplify an object with and without its augment vowel:

(10) a. Yohani si-a-nzire   o-mu-kali.
        John   NEG-1.s/T-like AUG-CL1-woman
        'John does not like the woman.'
     b. Yohani si-a-nzire   mu-kali.
        John   NEG-1.s/T-like CL1-woman
        'John does not like a(ny) woman.'

Whenever a noun lacks an augment vowel, it has an indefinite interpretation, as in (10b). Whenever a noun has an augment vowel, it is interpreted as definite, as indicated by the translation in (10a) (later we will see exceptions to this when the subject carries the augment vowel). A point relevant here is that an agreed-with phrase can never drop its augment vowel (Baker 2003), indicating that the agreed-with phrase must always be definite. By transitivity of reasoning, an indefinite phrase can only occur in a lower position, most typically in its originally merged position within vP/VP. In (11a), the subject has the augment vowel, whereas in (11b) it does not.

(11) a. O-mu-kali   mo-a-teta-gul-a   ki-ndu.
         AUG-CL1-woman AFF-1.S-NEG/PAST-buy-FV CL7-thing
         'The woman didn't buy anything.'
     b. *Mu-kali   mo-a-teta-gul-a   eritunda.
         CL1-woman AFF-1.S/T-NEG/PAST-buy-FV fruit.5
         'No woman bought a fruit.'

As (11b) shows, it is not possible for a phrase without the augment vowel, which is nonspecific and indefinite, to occur in the agreement position. What we have seen predicts that a completely nonspecific expression such as 'nobody' ought not be able to occur in the agreed-with position; Schneider-Zioga (2007:406) gives the following example as evidence that this is correct:

(12) *Si-ha-li   mundu eriyenda.
     NEG-there-be person CANONICAL-AGR.left
     'Nobody left.'

The augment-vowel phenomenon clearly shows that, in Kinande, something that occurs on the left edge is marked *both* as being the topic of the sentence *and* for agreement with the verbal inflection. Simply occupying the normal Spec,TP does not force a phrase to be interpreted as specific or definite. This topic interpretation arises from the phrase's moving to a higher region of the structure.

If we look at what Baker, Progovac, and Schneider-Zioga have observed about Kinande from the perspective of the Uniformity Principle interpreted as Strong Uniformity, which states that languages are entirely uniform, we are led to a picture of the language somewhat different from Baker's. Baker's analysis rests crucially on the idea that Case, particularly nominative Case, does not have any role to play in Kinande. But the Uniformity Principle/Strong Uniformity prescribes that Case ought to be present, and that it should have exactly the same role in this language as elsewhere in making arguments visible for θ-marking. Below, we will see instances where nominative Case emerges in Kinande exactly the way it emerges in languages where the function of Case is indisputable.

To begin, recall the primary insight in Baker's analysis of polysynthetic languages.

(13) A verb X agrees with an NP Y if and only if Y is in a dislocated, adjunct position.

As we saw, this property of dislocation is marked by the "topic" nature of the agreed-with phrase. What I propose is that this property of poly-synthetic languages identified by Baker, together with the seeming inert-ness of Case, points to the fact that the φ-probe in Kinande is inherited by a head higher than T, namely, α. α is not a Case assigner, so we would not expect the typical "nominative Case" effect with the φ-probe. But the φ-probe by itself cannot find a goal; to make this possible, −focus is also inherited by α, as shown in (14).

(14)

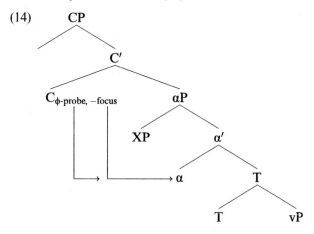

At the point where the φ-probe is inherited, it is not in any Agree relation. It enters such a relation only when an XP is raised to Spec,αP to satisfy the −focus feature. In this way, the polysynthetic biconditional that Baker observed falls out of the interactions of the grammatical features to-gether with a particular structure, αP, all consistent with the Uniformity Principle/Strong Uniformity.

I noted earlier that the αP projection does not always occur. If there are environments in Kinande where αP is disallowed, the φ-probe will be inherited by T instead of α. If that happens, we expect that Case will be-come a factor and that the φ-probe will only find the grammatical subject as its goal. Although Baker 2003 has no data bearing on this prediction, precisely the relevant situation turns up in *wh*-questions, as reported by Schneider-Zioga (2007), and in other, embedded contexts, as work with a native-speaker consultant, Pierre Mujomba, has revealed.

As noted by Progovac (1993), the agreed-with phrase in Kinande must be definite, reflecting its topic nature—a fact Baker (2003) draws upon extensively in his analysis. Thus, a nonspecific, nondefinite expression is inappropriate in this position.

(15) *Si-ha-li   mundu eriyenda.
      NEG-there-be person CANONICAL-AGR.left
      'Nobody left.'

Schneider-Zioga (2007) points out that this requirement that the agreed-with phrase must be definite is suspended if *wh*-movement takes place. (I have changed the verb form to *atahuka* from Schneider-Zioga's *syangahuka* at consultant Pierre Mujomba's suggestion.)

(16) Ekihi kyo mukali atahuka?
      what that woman not.cook
      'What didn't any woman cook?' (or 'What did no woman cook?')

Here the phrase 'woman' is interpreted as indefinite and nonspecific even though it agrees with the verb. Schneider-Zioga uses this fact to argue that the agreed-with phrase need not always move to a higher position, a conclusion with which I concur. Moreover, this lower phrase is limited to the subject, as I have confirmed with Pierre Mujomba.

(17) Iyondi yo   u-kandi-gul-a esyongoko?
      who   that AGR-will-buy the.chickens
      'Who will buy the chickens?'

(18) *Iyondi yo   esyongoko   si-kandi-gul-a?
       who   that the.chickens AGR-will-buy
      'Who will buy the chickens?'

Example (18) is an instance of object reversal, so the agreement goes with 'the chickens'. The fact that 'the chickens' is definite in (18) is not the problem, as other data from the consultant will show. I suggest that in certain environments, such as *wh*-questions, αP is not allowed to occur in Kinande, so that the φ-probe is inherited directly by T. Once this occurs, the φ-probe depends on the nominative Case of T and finds the grammatical subject, and nothing else, for its goal. This, then, is a clear indication that Case does matter in Kinande, contrary to Baker's (2003) analysis.[1]

We find the same restriction in relative clauses and clefts, which arguably also involve some sort of operator movement to C, apparently an environment where αP is not allowed. First, note the following declarative sentence:

(19) Abakali   ba-ka-gul-a esyongoko.
     the.women buy   chickens
     'The women buy chickens.'

The object reversal version of this sentence is (20), where the verb now
agrees with the object in the agreed-with position.

(20) Esyongoko si-ka-gul-a   bakali.
     the.chickens AGR-PRES-buy women
     'The WOMEN buy the chickens.'

Now, what happens to these sentences under relativization? It turns out
that they fare differently. In (21) and (22), the subject 'women' from (19)
and (20) has been relativized.

(21) abakali   ba-ka-gul-a esyongoko
     the.women buy   chickens
     'the women who buy the chickens'

(22) *abakali   esyongoko si-ka-gul-a
     the.women the.chickens buy
     'the women who buy the chickens'

This is the same pattern found with the *wh*-question (16) discussed by
Schneider-Zioga, but I have filled out the paradigm a bit more by showing that object reversal is not possible, demonstrating clearly that αP does
not occur if operator movement takes place. As a result, the φ-probe is
inherited by T, and because of T's dependence on nominative Case, only
the grammatical subject can be the goal, and it is the subject that is raised
to Spec,TP. Note, too, the following relative clauses:

(23) a. omulongo ogo   abakali   ba-ka-gul-a-ko   esyongoko
        the.village where the.women 3PL-PRES-buy-at/from the.chickens
        'the village where the women buy the chickens'
     b. omulongo ogo   bakali ba-ka-gul-a-ko   esyongoko
        the.village where women 3PL-PRES-buy-at/from the.chickens
        'the village where (some) women buy the chickens'

(24) a. omulongo ogo   esyongoko si-ka-gul-a-ko   bakali
        the.village where the.chickens AGR-PRES-buy-at women
        'the village where WOMEN buy the chickens'
     b. omulongo ogo   ngoko   si-ka-gul-a-ko   bakali
        the.village where chickens AGR-PRES-buy-at women
        'the village where WOMEN buy chickens'

Examples (23a–b) show again that the preverbal subject is fine whether it is definite or indefinite. What is surprising is that the two object reversal examples (24a–b) were judged acceptable by the consultant. Apparently these examples are interpreted not as relative clauses with operator movement, which would block αP and make the object reversal impossible, but as complex NPs, which arguably do not, or need not, involve operator movement. This demonstrates that just the consideration of informational structure (see note 1) cannot explain the pattern of grammaticality.

The following examples illustrate the restriction with clefts:

(25) Esyongoko esi   syo bakali ba-kandi-gul-a.
     chickens   these that women AGR-will-buy
     'It's these chickens that women will buy.'

(26) Abakali aba   bo   ba-kandi-gul-a esyongoko.
     women these that AGR-will-buy   the.chickens
     'It's these women who will buy the chickens.'

(27) *Abakali aba   bo   esyongoko   si-kandi-gul-a.
     women these that the.chickens AGR-will-buy
     'It's these women who will buy the chickens.'

The pattern of grammaticality in these operator-movement constructions—*wh*-question, relative clause, and cleft—suggests that nominative Case is a factor in Kinande.

4.3   Kilega *Wh*-Questions

Kilega is a Bantu language that resembles Kinande in many ways (Carstens 2005, Kinyalolo 1991). For example, the agreed-with phrase may be the subject, the object, or the locative. (All Kilega examples are taken from Carstens 2005, which in turn drew some of them from Kinyalolo 1991.)

(28) a. Mutu   t-á-ku-sol-ág-á   maku wéneéné.
        1person NEG-1AGR-PROG-A-sleep-FV 6beer alone
        'A person does not usually drink beer alone.'
     b. Maku ta-má-ku-sol-ág-á   mutu   wéneéné.
        6beer NEG-6AGR-PROG-drink-HAB-FV 1person alone
        'No one usually drinks beer alone.'
     c. Mu-zízo nyumbá mu-á-nyám-é   bána wálúbí.
        18-10-that 10house 18SA-A-sleep-FV 2child one.day.period
        'There will sleep children in those houses tomorrow.'

One difference between Kinande and Kilega is that in Kilega *wh*-questions, the fronted *wh*-phrase is what the verb agrees with. Examples (29)–(31) illustrate subject, object, and locative *wh*-phrase fronting in Kilega. (I will return to why the subject agreement *á* in (29) is not possible. The gloss CA stands for *complementizer agreement*, which I will also discuss below.)

(29) Nází ú-(*á)-ku-kít-ag-a   búbo?
     1who 1CA-(*1SA)-PROG-do-HAB-F-FV 14that
     'Who (usually) does that?'

(30) *Bikí bí-á-kás-il-é   bábo bíkulu mwámi mu-muwílo?
     8what 8CA-A-give-PERF-FV 2that 2woman 1chief   18-3village
     'What did those women give the chief in the village?'

(31) Kúní   *ku*-ta-*bá*-ku-yan-ág-á   mukindi?
     16where 16CA-NEG-2SA-PROG-play-HAB-FV 18-7night
     'Where don't they usually play at night?'

Two additional points are relevant to our discussion of *wh*-questions. First, Kilega (and also Kinande) has the *wh*-in-situ option; (32) is the in-situ counterpart of (30).

(32) Bábo bíkulu   b-á-kás-il-é   mwámi *bikí*   mu-muwílo?
     2that 2woman 2SA-A-give-PERF-FV 1chief   8what 18-3village
     'What did those women give the chief in the village?'

I will return to the in-situ option. Second, in an example like (30), where the verb agrees with the fronted object *wh*-phrase, the verb cannot also carry subject agreement.

(33) *Bikí   bí-b-á-kás-il-é   bábo bíkulu mwámi mu-muwílo?
     8what 8CA-2SA-A-give-PERF-FV 2that 2woman 1chief   18-3village
     'What did those women give the chief in the village?'

Therefore, as Carstens (2005) has argued, examples like (33) show that there can be only one formal agreement relation, and if a *wh*-phrase is to be moved, C must enter into agreement with the *wh*-phrase. Note, however, that it is not clear how we can accomplish this. In keeping with the analysis of Kinande proposed here, in the non-*wh* examples in (28) (the subject, the object, or the locative in the agreed-with position), the agreed-with phrase occupies Spec,αP. But α is not a head that hosts the feature relevant for *wh*-questions—namely, *wh* or Q, which we would expect to be borne instead on the higher head, C. I will sketch a possible analysis of the relevant portion of Kilega that distinguishes it from Kinande.

Let us suppose that the φ-probe is inherited by α in Kilega just as in Kinande. The difference is that unlike in Kinande, in Kilega αP may project in *wh*-questions. As a result, the *wh*-phrase can raise as the goal of the φ-probe on α. In Kinande, –focus is inherited together with the φ-probe, which gives rise to the topic interpretation of the goal. But a topic interpretation is inappropriate for a *wh*-phrase. How can the φ-probe on α be valued? Let us suppose that nothing else is inherited by α. Instead, there is a –focus feature on C that enters into an Agree relation with the *wh*-phrase, turning it into +focus, and this Agree relation requires the *wh*-phrase to raise ultimately to Spec,CP. However, on its way, the *wh*-phrase first merges with α and values the φ-probe (see (34)). Because the φ-probe and focus are different types of features, no Minimality violation ensues.

(34)

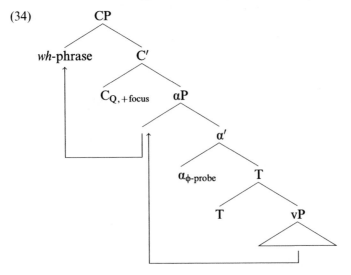

The first leg of the movement (to Spec,αP) values the φ-probe, and the second leg (to Spec,CP) places the *wh*-phrase properly in the domain of Q. This, then, shows that both topic and focus are relevant for the αP projection. The difference is that if –focus is inherited by α, it cannot be in a *wh*-question environment because there will be no way to raise the *wh*-phrase all the way to C.[2]

Note one crucial point here, however. Along with the movement of the *wh*-phrase, the α head must also raise to C. This is to ensure that at the next phase, when the interior of that higher phase is transferred to PF and semantic interpretation, the *wh*-phrase and its probes—focus and φ-probe—are in a "Spec-head" relation, thus fulfilling the probe-goal union (PGU) requirement. The idea that α raises is consistent with the Kilega data found in Carstens 2005. The agreement element has a different shape depending on whether it is pronounced at C or lower (α in the present analysis). I repeat example (29), which illustrates this.

(35) Nází ú-(*á)-ku-kít-ag-a   búbo?
     1who 1CA-(*1SA)-PROG-do-HAB-F-FV 14that
     'Who (usually) does that?'

In this *wh*-question, the *wh*-phrase agrees in class with the agreement element in the verbal morphology. Crucially, this agreement element is *ú*, not *á*. *Ú* is the agreement element for class 1 when the agreement element (and the verbal complex that contains it) occurs at C, whereas *á* is the agreement element for class 1 when the verbal complex occurs lower (α in the present analysis) (Carstens 2003, Kinyalolo 1991). The latter case is illustrated here (from Carstens 2005:265).

(36) Mutu   t-á-ku-sol-ág-á   maku wéneéne.
     1person NEG-1SA-PROG-drink-HAB-FV 6beer alone
     'A person does not usually drink beer alone.'

In this way, α is *raised* to C, after being picked up by the verbal complex, so that the entire verbal complex is at C. This meets the PGU requirement with the *wh*-phrase in Spec,CP. This is why the verbal complex always immediately follows the *wh*-phrase in Spec,CP.

Finally, if a non-*wh* phrase instead of the *wh*-phrase were raised to Spec,αP, the result would be an in-situ construction of the type we saw earlier in (32). In a *wh*-in-situ construction, the verbal complex does not raise to C; hence, the agreement is of the "lower" type, not the type that occurs at C.

(37) *Miwána ú-ku-kí-ag-a   bikí?
      1child 1CA-PROG-do-HAB-FV 2what
      'What does a/the child usually do?'

The agreement element should be the "lower" one, *á*, but instead *ú* occurs, the agreement element for class 1 at C. Finally, in the *wh*-in-situ construction, the φ-probe at α finds its goal thanks to −focus, which is also inherited by α.

4.4 Finnish

We saw in chapter 3 that Finnish has a topic projection above TP and below CP, which I labeled αP (in contrast to F[in]P in Holmberg and Nikanne 2002).[3]

(38) a. Graham Greene on kirjoittanut tämän kirjan.
        Graham Greene has written   this   book
        'Graham Greene has written this book.'
     b. Tämän kirjan on kirjoittanut Graham Greene.
        this   book has written   Graham Greene

As we saw in chapter 3, in both cases here the subject is 'Graham
Greene'. However, the topics differ: the subject 'Graham Greene' occupies topic position in (38a), but the object 'this book' occupies topic position in (38b).

(39) a. [$_{CP}$[$_{\alpha P}$ Graham Greene [$_{TP}$ ... this book ...]]]
     b. [$_{CP}$[$_{\alpha P}$ this book [$_{TP}$ ... Graham Greene ...]]]

Up to this point, Finnish looks very much like Kinande and Kilega in
having the αP projection that hosts a topic. Holmberg and Nikanne
(2002) go into some detail to show that the subject and the object in these
examples occupy the same position. For example, (40a–c) demonstrate
that a subject or an object in topic position can control a subject floating
quantifier, but a phrase in Spec,CP, which is higher than the topic, cannot
(Holmberg and Nikanne 2002:88).

(40) a. Ilmeisesti kriitikot   ovat (kaikki) ylsäneet tätä kirjaa.
        evidently the.critics have all   praised this book
     b. Ilmeisesti nämä kirjat on (kaikki) kirjoittanut Graham Greene.
        evidently these books has all   written   Graham Greene
        'Evidently Graham Greene has written all these books.'
     c. Nämä kirjat Graham Greene on (*kaikki) kirjoittanut (kaikki).
        these books Graham Greene has all   written   all

The subject (40a) and object (40b) in topic position can control the floating quantifier 'all' in the subject position immediately after the auxiliary
verb. What (40c) shows is that 'these books', which occurs in Spec,CP,
cannot control the subject floating quantifier; instead, it is limited to con-
trolling the postverbal floating quantifier.

Finnish differs from Kinande and Kilega in agreement possibilities. In
the Bantu languages, agreement may hold with the subject, object, or
locative. This led us to postulate that the ϕ-probe is inherited by α in this
language, not T, and that this ϕ-probe at α finds its goal through topicalization, the latter implemented by the –focus feature that also lowers to α
from C. In Finnish, despite its similarity with Bantu in topicalization possibilities, agreement always goes with the subject. Given our assumptions
about the ϕ-probe, this means that, unlike in the Bantu languages, in

Finnish the ɸ-probe is inherited by T, not α, as shown in (41). The ɸ-probe finds its goal through the nominative Case of T, which limits the goal to the nominative phrase. Presumably, the –focus feature is inherited by α, just as in the Bantu languages.

(41)

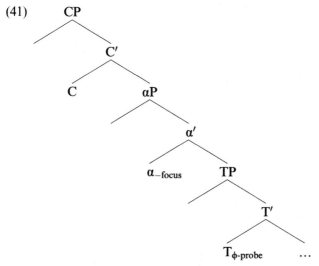

The ɸ-probe seeks its goal while at T, as in (41), but the T bearing this ɸ-probe ultimately shows up on α, presumably raising there with other relevant material (Holmberg and Nikanne 2002:72). One argument for this involves *pro*-drop (Holmberg 2005:539).

(42) a. (Minä) puhun   englantia.
          I   speak.1sG English
     b. (Sinä) puhut   englantia.
          you   speak.2sG English
     c. *(Hän) puhuu   englantia.
          he/she speak.3sG English
     d. (Me) puhumme englantia.
          we   speak.1PL English
     e. (Te) puhutte   englantia.
          you speak.2PL English
     f. *(He) puhuvat   englantia.
          they speak.3PL English

As shown, the verb 'speak' with the appropriate agreement occurs next to where the *pro* is postulated to occur. Moreover, first and second person agreement, but not third, licenses *pro* in this language. Recall from chapter 3 that the expletive *sitä* is merged at Spec,αP to satisfy the –focus feature, not the φ-probe. The relevant example is (43), from Holmberg and Nikanne 2002:72.

(43) Sitä ovat nämä lapset   jo   oppineet uimaan.
     EXPL have these children already learned   to.swim
     'These children have already learned to swim.'

Sitä is a "pure" expletive in that it is not related to φ-features or Case (Holmberg and Nikanne 2002:90). The topic position is not just a position relevant to information structure; it imparts a subjectlike quality to any element that appears in it, even an object. Returning to *pro*-drop, we see that the expletive *sitä* and *pro* are incompatible (Holmberg 2005:543).

(44) *Sitä puhun   englantia.
     EXPL speak.1SG English

Holmberg argues that this indicates that the *pro* occurs in topic position, what I am calling αP. Since *pro* occurs in topic position, the expletive *sitä* cannot also occur there.

The similarities and differences between the Bantu languages we looked at earlier and Finnish are clear: both have the αP projection, which in declarative sentences hosts a topic, but the φ-probe occurs in different positions. In the Bantu languages, the φ-probe is inherited by α, whereas in Finnish, it is inherited by T. This difference leads to differences in agreement possibilities, including licensing of *pro*. Despite this difference, agreement (the head with the φ-probe) occurs at α in both cases, the φ-probe having been inherited directly by α in the Bantu languages, and T with the φ-probe having raised to α in Finnish. This is all consistent with the type of approach developed here so far. The one inconsistency has to do with the fact that in Finnish, it is apparently possible for a nongoal as well as the goal to occur in Spec,αP. Recall (38b), repeated here.

(45) Tämän kirjan on kirjoittanut Graham Greene.
     this   book has written   Graham Greene

In this example, agreement goes with the subject, 'Graham Greene', and it shows up on the auxiliary verb *on* 'has' at α. Surprisingly, the object 'this book' occurs in Spec,αP as the topic even though *on* agrees with the subject; the subject occurs low in the structure, as we can see. This is an exception to the idea that a functional relation established by Agree must be replicated by movement of the goal to the probe before transfer to interpretation.

What causes this failure of correlation between φ-probe and PGU? To repeat the problem, in Finnish the φ-probe always enters into agreement with the subject, indicating that the φ-probe occurs on T at the point where agreement is established. Yet the φ-probe ultimately moves to α, and the subject may or may not move with it. If it does not, it fails to fulfill the PGU requirement. Why is it able to ignore PGU? What appears to be happening in Finnish is that functional relations such as topic and subject-of are established not by φ-feature agreement, although it occurs, but by the topic structure (–focus). So, for example, it is topic position that allows control of the subject floating quantifier regardless of whether the subject or the object occurs in the topic position. The φ-feature agreement appears to be a strictly surface matter. The combination of Case and φ-features requires that agreement be implemented so that the features that need to be erased before being transferred can be erased. But because the functional relations that are retained beyond the interface are those established by the topic feature, the relations established by φ-feature agreement do not have any role to play beyond establishing agreement. Hence, the goal of the agreement need not move to the probe to fulfill PGU, and this relation is erased prior to transfer. It is possible that φ-feature agreement does have a role to play after transfer just in those cases where PGU is met—when the subject moves into topic position. I will leave this issue open.

4.5 Distinguishing A- and Ā-Movements without Reference to Case

We saw in the discussion of Kilega that the PGU requirement holds regardless of whether the movement that takes place is A- or Ā-movement. This is, in fact, what we wish to see: the condition(s) for movement ought to be the same for all movements that are triggered by a probe-goal relation, and this relation should hold for both A- and Ā-movements. I assume that all probes begin at a phase head such as C; if the probe is inherited by T, movement stops at T, but a probe that is retained at C triggers movement to the C domain. As far as probe-goal relations for movement are concerned, this is essentially all that narrow syntax provides. But if the triggering mechanism (probe-goal) does not distinguish A- and Ā-movements, how *are* they distinguished? We saw clear evidence in chapter 3 that these two movements behave differently. A-movement can overcome WCO violations and can create a new binder, but Ā-movement can do neither. It is also well known that while A-movement can overcome a Condition C violation, in most cases Ā-movement cannot.

These three facts about the two types of movement—WCO suppression, creation of a new binder, and Condition C suppression—are typically viewed in the context of reconstruction: although A-movement does not need to undergo reconstruction, Ā-movement typically does. This is often characterized in terms of A-movement not being required to leave a (full) copy in the original position and Ā-movement leaving such a copy. Fox (1999) and Lasnik (1999a) describe it in terms of Ā-traces being copies and A-traces being unstructured. (*Unstructured* simply means that something is there but is not a fully specified copy.) Lasnik (1999a, 2003) has argued that A-movement never leaves a (full) copy. Nevertheless, I will follow other works (e.g., Fox 1999 and references therein) that suggest that A-movement allows reconstruction—hence is allowed to leave a full copy, although it is not required to do so—but that Ā-movement always leaves a full copy.

4.5.1   A- and Ā-Movements

A typical case of reconstruction associated with Ā-movement is (46) (based on an example from Fox 1999:172).

(46) [Which of his$_i$ students] do you think [every professor]$_i$ talked to?

We can see that this construal is mediated by movement from the fact that (47) (also based on an example from Fox 1999:172) is ungrammatical with the intended interpretation.

(47) *[Which of his$_i$ students] do you think talked to [every professor]$_i$?

In the grammatical example (46), the *wh*-phrase containing the pronoun begins in a position lower than the universal expression *every professor*; but in the ungrammatical example (47), the *wh*-phrase starts out higher than the universal expression. Example (46) is an instance of reconstruction, and in the copy theory of movement (Chomsky 1993, 1995), this means that a full copy of the *wh*-phrase occurs in the original position.

(48) [which of his students] do you think [every professor] talked to
     [which of his students]

It is the lower copy that allows the pronoun inside it to be bound by the universal expression. No such copy exists lower than the universal quantifier in (47).

The occurrence of the copy in (46) allows the pronoun inside the *wh*-phrase to be bound by the universal quantifier, but there are instances where the copy leads to ungrammaticality. Relevant examples were noted by Freidin (1986) and Van Riemsdijk and Williams (1981); (49a–b) come from Freidin 1986:179.

(49) a. *[Which report that John$_i$ was incompetent] did he$_i$ submit?
     b. [Which report that John$_i$ revised] did he$_i$ submit?

In (49a), the copy of the Ā-movement contains the R-expression *John* and it is c-commanded by the pronoun with which it is coindexed, triggering a Condition C violation. This is what we expect if Ā-movement obligatorily leaves a copy. I will return to (49b), which is unexpectedly grammatical even though it also involves Ā-movement.

Turning to A-movement, we see from (50) that, like Ā-movement, A-movement allows reconstruction (example from Fox 1999:161).

(50) [Someone from his$_i$ class] seems to [every professor]$_i$ to be a genius.

However, unlike Ā-movement, A-movement is apparently not forced to leave a copy, as the following examples show ((51a) from Chomsky 1993:37); ((51b) from Lebeaux 1988:23).

(51) a. [The claim that John$_i$ was asleep] seems to him$_i$ to be correct.
     b. [John$_i$'s mother] seems to him$_i$ to be wonderful.

These examples do not show a Condition C violation, which indicates that A-movement does not leave a copy in the relevant sense. The generalization to be drawn for the two types of movement is this (Takahashi 2006, Takahashi and Hulsey 2009):

(52) a. A-movement optionally leaves a copy.
     b. Ā-movement obligatorily leaves a copy.

4.5.2 Takahashi 2006 and Takahashi and Hulsey 2009

To capture the generalizations in (52), Takahashi (2006) and Takahashi and Hulsey (2009) (henceforth TTH) propose an interesting theory of the two types of movement. I will briefly introduce their approach, then show a problem with it, and finally propose an alternative that overcomes the problem.

TTH's central idea is that *late Merge* (Lebeaux 1988; see also Chomsky 1993) applies widely in grammar. What is late Merge? Recall Freidin's (1986:179) pair in (49), repeated here.

(53) a. *[Which report that John$_i$ was incompetent] did he$_i$ submit?
     b. [Which report that John$_i$ revised] did he$_i$ submit?

Example (53a) is ungrammatical, as expected, because this is an instance of Ā-movement, which obligatorily leaves a full copy that, in this case, triggers a Condition C violation. But what about (53b)? Lebeaux (1988) argues that the difference between these two examples arises from the fact that, whereas (53a) contains a full copy of the entire *wh*-phrase, in (53b) the copy consists only of the head of the relative clause and the *wh*-element (*which report*); the relative clause *that John revised* does not occur in the lower copy. The notion that Lebeaux introduced to account for examples like (53b) is *late Merge*, which allows some unit of expression to be merged into the structure countercyclically. Specifically, in (53b), the relative clause *that John revised* is introduced by late Merge into the *wh*-phrase, after the *wh*-phrase has moved to Spec,CP. Prior to movement, the structure includes only *which report*, and because this does not contain the R-expression, there is no Condition C violation. Why is late Merge not possible in (53a)? Lebeaux argues that in (53a), the expression that contains the R-expression (*that John was incompetent*) is the argument of the head *report*, and as such, it must have been merged with the head to begin with; as a result, the entire *wh*-phrase, including the R-expression, occurs in the original position of the *wh*-phrase. But in (53b), the relative clause is an adjunct, and adjuncts need not be merged initially with their head. Instead, they can be merged late, avoiding a Condition C violation.

Following the suggestion of Bhatt and Pancheva (2004, 2007), TTH argue that late Merge is a more widespread phenomenon than Lebeaux first proposed. They argue that the "bleeding" of Condition C demonstrated for A-movement in examples like (51a–b) indicates that a type of late Merge has occurred (I repeat (51a) here). In fact, TTH propose that a structure bigger than what Lebeaux suggested may be introduced by late Merge; they call this process *wholesale late merger*.

(54) [The claim that John$_i$ was asleep] seems to him$_i$ to be correct.

Extending the analysis of late Merge in Fox 2002, TTH suggest that in one derivation, which results in a grammatical sentence with the intended interpretation, only the D, *the*, and its projection, DP, are merged at the base. This *the* is the target of raising, and after raising takes place, the matrix Spec,TP hosts just this *the*. To this DP in Spec,TP, the NP structure *claim that John was asleep* is merged by wholesale late merger. The lower copy consists of just D/DP *the*, which makes it possible to avoid a Condition C violation.

TTH extend this idea of wholesale late merger to well-known examples of quantifier scope noted by May (1977).

(55) Some argument seems to be correct.

This sentence has one reading in which there exists an argument that seems to be correct (*some argument* > *seem*) and another reading in which it seems that some argument is correct (*seem* > *some argument*). The second reading involves reconstruction. What TTH argue is that in the first reading, which does not involve reconstruction, wholesale late merger takes place in the following way. For the first reading associated with (55), the lower clause has the representation *[some] correct*. This *some* raises to Spec,TP, resulting in the structure (56a).[4] To this, wholesale late merger applies and inserts the restrictor *argument*, as in (56b).

(56) a.

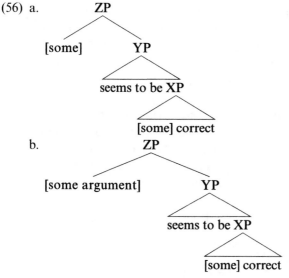

This structure does not have the NP *argument* in the lower copy; hence, the reconstruction effect is absent. The lower copy does receive some interpretation; TTH suggest that this "small" copy undergoes Fox's (2002) Trace Conversion for proper interpretation (see TTH 2006, 2009 for details). For the reconstruction interpretation of (55), *argument* is merged to begin with, as shown in (57); in semantic interpretation, it is this lower full copy that gets interpreted.

(57)

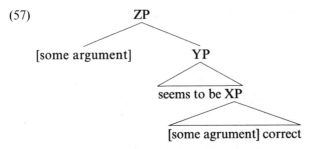

Given that both A- and Ā-movements allow late Merge, how do we distinguish between the two in a way that captures the observation that A-movement leaves a copy optionally but Ā-movement does so obligatorily? TTH make the point that a copy is obligatorily left in both types of movement. For example, in (56a) *some* is merged as the subject of *correct*, and it is left as the copy of the movement. The difference arises from the particular positions that allow late Merge. For this, TTH turn to considerations of Case (Chomsky 1981), arguing that in a DP structure, both the DP and the NP inside it require Case. In *wh*-movement, which is Ā-movement, the landing site is a non-Case position so that if an NP is introduced by wholesale late merger into the DP that has been *wh*-moved, the NP will be without Case. On the other hand, the landing site of A-movement is a Case position, so that an NP that is introduced into the moved DP by wholesale late merger will receive Case. Hence, A-movement always allows the possibility of wholesale late merger, and this is why it appears that A-movement only optionally leaves a copy.

4.5.3 A Problem with TTH's Proposal, and a Solution: Phase-Based Characterization of Chains

TTH's proposal can account for the core data regarding A- and Ā-movements in English. A problem arises when we look beyond English, however. As we saw earlier, in scrambling languages such as Hindi and Japanese, A-movement scrambling can overcome WCO, and it can also create a new binder, both indicating that a full copy is not present in the original position. Yet the movement involved is clearly not driven by Case since typical A-movement scrambling takes the object and puts it to the left of the subject. The following examples are repeated from chapter 3:

(58) a. *[Kinoo   *pro*$_i$ *pro*$_j$ atta hito$_i$]-ga   dare-o$_j$ hihansita no?
          yesterday   met person-NOM who-ACC criticized Q
          Lit. 'The person who met (him) yesterday criticized whom?'

b. Dare-o$_j$ [kinoo   *pro*$_i$ *pro*$_j$ atta hito$_i$]-ga t_j hihansita no?
who-ACC yesterday   met person-NOM   criticized Q
Lit. 'Who, the person who met (him) yesterday criticized?'

Example (58a) is a straightforward WCO violation; 'who-ACC' fails to c-command the *pro* inside the subject phrase. In (58b), this object 'who-ACC' has scrambled by A-movement to a position that c-commands the *pro*, allowing the sentence to overcome a WCO violation (e.g., Hoji 1985, Saito 1992). This movement of the object to the head of the sentence clearly doesn't happen for Case reasons, yet it has the same "no copy" property as the A-movement in English that targets a Case position. How can we capture the optional nature of the lower copy in A-movement and its obligatoriness in Ā-movement without reference to Case?

I will propose a solution based on the phase architecture of narrow syntax. According to this view, structures are built from the bottom up in chunks, called phases. The phases that have been identified are vP and CP (and possibly DP). Once a phase is completed, its complement (or "interior") is transferred to PF and to semantic interpretation, leaving the edge of the phase to be transferred with the complement of the next higher phase (Chomsky 2001, 2005, 2007, 2008). Ultimately, the phases have to be put back together in PF and at semantic interpretation to make the sentence whole, and this is where I suggest that the A/Ā distinction with respect to copies come into play. Let us suppose that chains are characterized as follows:

(59) *Phase-based characterization of chains*
A full copy of a moved item must be available for interpretation if the movement crosses a transfer domain boundary.

The idea is simple, and the two possibilities are illustrated in (60).

(60) a.

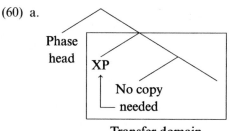

Transfer domain

b.

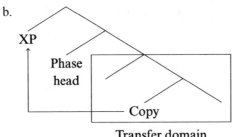

Transfer domain

The intuitive idea is that when it comes time to put the phases back together in semantic interpretation, a chain must be made whole, and if a chain is dispersed between two phases (or *transfer domains*, more accurately), a record of the chain in its entirety must be kept. In other words, a full copy of the moved element must be present. If the movement occurs within the same transfer domain, the chain as a whole is transferred intact, so there is no need for a fully specified copy to occur at the point where the movement originated, although there is nothing wrong with leaving such a copy. With this in mind, let us look concretely at three cases (*NCN* stands for *no copy needed*).

(61) *Movement of a DP to Spec,TP from vP*
     [$_{CP}$[$_{TP}$ DP [$_{vP}$ NCN [$_{VP}$ ...]]]]

(62) *Raising*
     [$_{TP}$ DP [seem [$_{TP}$ NCN ...]]]

(63) Wh-*movement*
     [$_{CP}$ wh-phrase [$_{TP}$ ... [$_{vP}$ wh-phrase [$_{vP}$ ... [$_{VP}$ wh-phrase ...]]]]]

The movement illustrated in (61) could be the movement of the external argument to Spec,TP, or it could be the scrambling of the object (or some other VP-internal XP) to the TP domain. The movement illustrated in (62) is raising. In these two cases, the movement takes place within the same transfer domain so that a copy isn't needed, though there's always the option of leaving a full copy. In the case of raising, I assume that the matrix v is defective and does not form a phase (Chomsky 2001); the same analysis applies to A-movement in passives. *Wh*-movement, illustrated in (63), does cross a transfer domain boundary—in fact, two (VP,

TP), because the *wh*-phrase here is an object *wh*-phrase—so a copy must be available in each domain for re-creating the sentence as a whole at semantic interpretation. Note that whether a copy is needed or not can be evaluated at each phase level, avoiding look-ahead. To summarize: Once a phase is built—say, CP—if it contains a chain formed by movement, a copy is left to be interpreted if the chain crosses the transfer domain boundary—the complement of the phase. Otherwise, a copy is unnecessary.

In TTH's system, late Merge is intimately connected to Case. Late Merge (wholesale late merger) is always possible with instances of A-movement because A-movements terminate at a Case position, and the Case licenses the NP that is introduced into the moved DP by late Merge. With instances of Ā-movement, late Merge of an NP is impossible because Ā-movements do not terminate at a Case position. Although this picture is plausible if the data are limited to English, we saw that once we bring in A-movement scrambling, Case considerations must be set aside. But if that is true, the possibility arises that late Merge can also be set aside for A-movement. Everything else being equal, that would be desirable given that late Merge violates two principles, Cyclicity and the Extension Condition. It may still be right, but if we can do without it, the design of narrow syntax would be simpler. I will suggest this for A-movement, leaving open the question of whether late Merge can also be eliminated in Ā-movement.

Under the phase-based characterization of chains (PBCC), there is no reason to assume the late Merge model for A-movement; instead, we can go back to the simpler view that A-movement optionally leaves a copy. With the PBCC, we need not make any reference to A-movement versus Ā-movement. Instead, any movement that does not cross a transfer domain boundary is free to not leave a copy (although it can), whereas a movement that crosses a transfer domain boundary must leave a copy so that the chain can be put back together in the semantic component.

There is another point we need to observe about A-movement. Let us suppose that a movement that occurs strictly within a transfer domain leaves a copy. In TTH's approach, this leads to reconstruction, which means that the higher copy is not interpreted. But is this true? A simpler view is that even in these cases of "reconstruction," the higher copy, which is the pronounced one, is capable of being interpreted as well. The following example from Japanese demonstrates this point:[5]

(64) [Dono zibun$_i$-no e]-o$_j$ [e$_j$ sore$_j$-o kaita] ekaki$_i$-ga t_j
     which self-GEN   picture-ACC   it-ACC   drew   artist-NOM
     kiratteiru no?
     hate   Q
     'Which of self's pictures does the artist who drew it hate?'

In this example, the object *wh*-phrase has scrambled locally to the left of
the subject. This *wh*-phrase binds the pronoun *sore* 'it' inside the relative
clause modifying the subject 'artist'. The pronoun does not c-command
the trace of the moved *wh*-phrase, yet this binding construal is possible,
which indicates that we are dealing with an A-movement, and the *wh*-
phrase is interpreted at the moved position above the subject. At the
same time, the *wh*-phrase contains the anaphor *zibun* 'self', which is
bound by the subject 'artist'; this requires that the copy of the A-moved
wh-phrase must also be interpreted in its original position below the
subject. Clearly, in this example, the lower copy is available for interpretation even though the movement took place wholly within a transfer domain. The simplest way to view this sort of movement is to say that the
higher copy is always available for interpretation, and the lower copy, if
left, can also be interpreted. As (65) shows, without this movement, the
sentence is ungrammatical because it violates WCO, as expected.

(65) *[e$_j$ Sore$_j$-o kaita] ekaki$_i$-ga [dono zibun$_i$-no e]-o$_j$
        it-ACC   drew   artist-NOM which self-GEN   picture-ACC
     kiratteiru no?
     hate   Q
     'Which of self's pictures does the artist who drew it hate?'

Of the several native speakers I consulted, all found (64) fine, although
one hesitated until a proper context could be imagined, in which the artist
drew many pictures of himself. Judgments for (65) ranged from ungrammatical to marginal (* to ??), which is typical of WCO violations. Finally,
the English version of (64) evidences exactly the same property: both
copies are available for interpretation simultaneously.[6]

(66) [No picture of him$_i$]$_j$ seems to every student$_i$ who drew it$_i$ t_j to be
     nice.

Just as with the Japanese example (64), it takes a moment to imagine
an appropriate context for (66)—one in which each student drew many
pictures of himself—but once we can do so, the sentence appears to be
grammatical with the intended reading in which the A-moved quantifier
phrase *no picture of him* binds the pronoun *it* from the moved position,

and the pronoun *him* inside this quantifier is bound in the lower copy by the quantifier *every student*.

Next, I will return to Finnish and show how the PBCC approach to A- and Ā-movement correctly accounts for an unusual "mixed" position.

4.5.4 A "Mixed" Position in Finnish

The constructions we have observed so far are fairly conventional for the most part, and there are surely other ways to account for them. What the PBCC predicts, however, is the existence of some exotic movements whose landing sites combine the properties of A- and Ā-positions. Such a movement is found in Finnish (Holmberg and Nikanne 2002:87); see É. Kiss 1995:233 for a similar example in Hungarian. In Finnish, there is a topic position above TP. In chapter 3, I labeled this as *αP*, but for the sake of the exposition here, I will use *Top(ic)P*. The following example is judged grammatical by Holmberg and Nikanne:

(67) Ilmeisesti itseää   äänesti vain Jussi.
     apparently for.himself voted   only Jussi
     'Apparently the only person who voted for himself was Jussi.'

The odd property of this example is that an anaphor occurs in a topic position, which Holmberg and Nikanne clearly identify as an A-position, not an Ā-position—yet it must also be an Ā-position because the anaphor must reconstruct. As a result, Holmberg and Nikanne characterize this topic position as a *mixed* A- and Ā-position. This is an example where A-movement allows the higher copy to be interpreted even though the lower copy must also be interpreted: the higher copy receives an interpretation such that 'for.himself' is given a topic reading in the moved position. Its lower copy also must receive an interpretation, for the obvious reason.

The fact that 'for.himself' occupies an A-position is indicated by the fact that a phrase in this position (whether subject or object) can control a subject floating quantifier. Recall (40a–c), repeated here.

(68) a. Ilmeisesti kriitikot ovat (kaikki) ylsäneet tätä kirjaa.
        evidently the.critics have all   praised this book
     b. Ilmeisesti nämä kirjat on (kaikki) kirjoittanut Graham Greene.
        evidently these books has all   written   Graham Greene
        'Evidently Graham Greene has written all these books.'
     c. Nämä kirjat Graham Greene on (*kaikki) kirjoittanut (kaikki).
        these books Graham Greene has all   written   all

Although the subject (68a) and the object (68b) in the topic position can control the subject floating quantifier, which occurs between the auxiliary and the verbal participle, a phrase in Spec,CP cannot do so (68c).

The PBCC makes the correct prediction without resorting to a "mixed" position.

(69) *Object topicalization*

$$[_{CP} \ldots [_{TopP} \text{XP}_{Obj} [_{TP} \ldots [_{vP} \text{NCN} \ldots [_{VP} \ldots \text{XP} \ldots]]]]]$$

The first leg of the movement crosses the transfer domain boundary, VP. As a result, a copy must be left in the original position, which accounts for the reconstruction effect. The second leg of the movement occurs within the same transfer domain, from the edge of vP to TopP. Hence, this second piece of the chain has the option of leaving or not leaving a copy. Even if the lower copy is not interpreted, the higher copy, which is in the same transfer domain as this lower copy, can be construed with the full copy that has been left in the original, object position in the previous transfer domain. The series of movements just described would constitute an improper movement in the traditional approach since the first is Ā-movement, and this is followed by A-movement. Under the present analysis, there is nothing wrong with this movement; this analysis makes no reference to the A or Ā nature of movement, and Case is properly assigned to the lower copy but not the higher copy given that the last movement does not terminate in a Case position. This sequence of chains that terminates at Spec,TopP has two copies, one in Spec,TopP, and the other in the original position of the moved item. Both copies receive interpretation: the copy in Spec,TopP, which associates the anaphor with a topic interpretation, and the copy in the original object position, which makes it possible for the anaphor to be bound by its antecedent. Finally, in those cases where the object in Spec,TopP controls a subject floating quantifier, no copy is left at the edge of vP, and no reconstruction takes place.

As the final point in this chapter, recall from chapter 3 that the following examples show that the object in Japanese may scramble to Spec,TP and allow the subject to stay in Spec,vP (Miyagawa 2001):

(70) a. Zen'in-ga siken-o uke-nakat-ta.
        all-NOM   test-ACC take-NEG-PAST
        'All did not take the test.'
        all > not, */??not > all

b. Siken-o_i zen'in-ga t_i uke-nakat-ta.
test-ACC all-NOM take-NEG-PAST
'Test, all didn't take.'
all > not, not > all

In the SOV order in (70a), the preferred reading is for the subject 'all' to take wide scope over negation (Kato 1988); but in (70b), with the object scrambled, the partial negation interpretation becomes much easier for many speakers. I argued in Miyagawa 2001 that these examples indicate that in (70a) the subject has moved to Spec,TP, outside the domain of negation, whereas in (70b) it is the object that has moved to Spec,TP, allowing the subject to stay in Spec,vP and inside the scope of negation.

In response to this argument, Saito (2006) gives the following example:

(71) Zibun-zisin-o_i zen'in-ga t_i seme-nakat-ta.
self-self-ACC all-NOM blame-NEG-PAST
'Self, all didn't blame.'
all > not, not > all

As Saito correctly notes, it is possible to get the partial negation interpretation here, which indicates that the scrambled item is raised to Spec,TP by A-movement; but given that the scrambled item is an anaphor, it must be reconstructed, which in the traditional view means that the movement is in fact Ā-movement. Saito concludes that the effect that is identified in Miyagawa 2001 as partial negation is possible even with Ā-movement, hence that it has nothing to do with the EPP feature of T. Although this conclusion is well founded in the traditional view that ties reconstruction solely to Ā-movement, we have seen that, under the PBCC, A-movement can also take part in reconstruction, with concomitant interpretation of the higher copy. Under this view, in (71), the anaphor has moved to Spec,TP, where it meets the requirement that I earlier called the EPP and now would call topicalization. But at the same time, its copy in VP, which is a transfer domain, is also interpreted and the anaphor is properly bound by the subject 'all'.

One question that arises concerns (70a), which indicates that in the SOV order, the universal subject that has undergone A-movement from Spec,vP to Spec,TP does not reconstruct, making it difficult to get a partial negation interpretation.[8] Under the PBCC approach, it ought to be possible for the subject to leave a copy in Spec,vP; hence, a partial negation interpretation should emerge. One possible reason why it doesn't is that, as extensively discussed in chapter 3, this particular movement is conditioned by either topic or focus, and, at least for focus, it has been shown that the focused element must be interpreted in its surface position (É. Kiss 1998). I will assume that the lack of a copy in this instance is not an exception to the PBCC, but instead results from a particular factor surrounding the movement, such as topic/focus.

4.6 Summary

In the first part of this chapter, I explored the consequence for the current approach when both −focus (topic) and the φ-probe are inherited by α. Given that the φ-probe does not lower to T, it does not interact with nominative Case. But because a φ-probe must depend on something else, in this case −focus, to identify its goal, the current approach predicts that the goal of the φ-probe can be any appropriate DP and not just the subject, and it must always be a topic that occurs in Spec,αP. This is what we found for Kinande and Kilega, two languages from the Bantu family. We also found that in certain instances—apparently those that have operator movement—Kinande does not allow the αP projection. This forces the φ-probe to be inherited by T. This, in turn, led to a very different pattern of agreement in which the goal of the agreement is limited to the grammatical subject because the φ-probe depends on nominative Case on T to seek its goal. We also looked at wh-question formation in Kilega. Kilega has the unusual property that, in wh-questions, agreement goes with the wh-phrase at Spec,CP. I analyzed this as a case in which the focus probe (−focus turned into +focus under agreement) agrees with the wh-phrase and moves the wh-phrase up to Spec,CP, but on its way the wh-phrase stops by Spec,αP to value the φ-probe on α.

Another language that has both topic/focus and φ-feature agreement is Finnish. However, as we saw, Finnish works differently from Kinande and Kilega in one important respect. Unlike in the Bantu languages, in Finnish the φ-probe is always inherited by T, so that agreement always goes with the subject. The topic feature (−focus) is inherited by α just as in the Bantu languages, but because the topic feature and the φ-probe are on different heads, Finnish allows a topic to occur in Spec,αP that is not the goal of the φ-probe, such as the object.

In the second half of the chapter, I outlined a theory of A- and Ā-movements that I called the phase-based characterization of chains (PBCC). According to this approach, we need not specify the landing site as an A- or Ā-position to predict whether a particular movement is A- or Ā-movement insofar as A-movement need not leave a fully specified copy whereas Ā-movement must. The PBCC addresses how the semantic interface must combine all the transfers that were sent to it into one whole sentence. The central issue is whether a movement has crossed a transfer domain boundary. For the two adjacent phases to be combined properly, a chain that crossed the transfer domain boundary must have a copy in the lower transfer domain, so that the tail of the chain can be properly linked with the head in the higher transfer domain. This gives the typical reconstruction effect. If, however, a movement takes place entirely within a transfer domain, there is no need for a copy, although there is always the option of leaving one. We saw that the PBCC can solve a problem that arises with the A/Ā analysis of Takahashi (2006) and Takahashi and Hulsey (2009), and it also provides an explanation for the exotic "mixed" position in Finnish.

5 *Wh*-Questions and Focus

5.1 *Wh*-Questions

In a *wh*-question, a question operator at C binds a bound variable. The bound variable itself is contained in the restriction term that defines the range of the objects that the bound variable may stand for (people, objects, etc.). Linguists typically represent this operator–bound variable relation as the Q feature on C binding the bound variable that is contained in the *wh*-phrase. Let us assume this. The question I wish to ask is, how does the Q feature come to bind the relevant element contained in the *wh*-phrase? It is commonly believed that the Q feature enters into an Agree relation with the relevant feature(s) of the *wh*-phrase (e.g., Baker 1970, Hagstrom 1998, Richards 2001), and this Agree relation makes the operator–bound variable interpretation possible. It also triggers, in some fashion that is not well understood, the movement of the *wh*-phrase to Spec,CP for those languages that have *wh*-movement.[1]

How does the Q feature manage to enter into an Agree relation with the *wh*-phrase? There is an assumption that it enters into Agree with an appropriate feature on the *wh*-phrase, something like a *wh*-feature. However, this is inconsistent with the recent Minimalist Program approach to Agree, including the approach taken here, because Agree presumes the existence of an uninterpretable feature, and there is no reason to believe that Q is an uninterpretable feature. The most sensible way to view it is as a fully interpretable feature that endows the expression with the speech-act force of interrogation.

We might take a different tack and account for the Q-variable relation as one of unselective binding. One leading assumption that could serve as the basis for this approach is to view the operator in a *wh*-question as an existential quantifier (Karttunen 1977). Heim (1982) proposes that the typical existential quantifiers (*some X*) are themselves not quantifiers;

. rather, they are bound variables of quantification. The actual existential quantifier occurs higher in the structure, and it unselectively binds the bound variable. This accounts for the surprising behavior of existentials, including the so-called donkey sentences. Karttunen, refining the approach to questions by Hamblin (1973), has argued that the quantification essential to questions is existential quantification. If we combine this view of *wh*-questions with the view of Tsai (1994) and Reinhart (1995) that the *wh*-operator, which may or may not be an existential, unselectively binds the *wh*-phrase to implement the operator-variable chain, we essentially get a Heim-style approach to quantification being applied to *wh*-questions. On this view, Q behaves like an uninterpretable feature without being one because it must (unselectively) bind a bound variable. Is this the correct way to view the Q feature? Certainly, the fact that it appears to be able to bind more than one *wh*-phrase, as in the multiple-*wh* construction (Baker 1970), makes the unselective binding approach credible.

There is one problem with the unselective binding approach: it does not explain why the *wh*-phrase must move to Spec,Q in some languages. In operator-variable chains, it is never required that the variable must move to the specifier of the head that hosts the operator. From the perspective taken here, the movement requirement in *wh*-questions (at least for the *wh*-movement languages) is not a matter of an operator-variable relation; rather, it points to the occurrence of a probe that attracts its goal (*wh*-phrase) by movement. By postulating such a probe for *wh*-questions, we can keep the Q feature as a pristine interpretable feature. The Q feature is not a probe, in other words. We can also account for the movement of *wh*-phrases. What goal feature could the probe seek in a *wh*-question? In the previous chapters, I gave ample evidence that in addition to φ-features, topic/focus is a probe available universally. I have assumed that this holds at the TP level. For *wh*-questions, we are looking at agreement at the CP level, but is there any reason to expand the range of possible goals and their features and the corresponding probe? Ideally, we would want to keep exactly the same possibilities: topic/focus features and φ-features. I will argue for this. Typically, *wh*-questions are associated with focus, and, as I will show, this is no accident. Not only is focus semantically compatible with *wh*-questions; it also happens to be one of the two common types of grammatical features available as a probe, the other being φ-features. We saw in chapter 4 how focus operates in *wh*-questions in Kilega, and the analysis in this chapter will apply that assumption to *wh*-questions in general.

In this chapter, I develop an analysis of *wh*-questions, paying particular attention to the mechanism that makes the Q-*wh* construal possible. As I will show, focus plays a central role in creating this linkage. Along with *wh*-questions, I take up the related issue of intervention, which Kim (2002, 2006) argues is induced by focus, a point also developed by Beck (2006). I will provide additional evidence for this focus approach to intervention based on my analysis of *wh*-questions.

To set the stage, let us begin by briefly looking at Watanabe's (2002) analysis of *wh*-movement in Old Japanese. This study, combined with Hagstrom 1998 and Miyagawa 2001, hints at the basic elements that go into *wh*-questions across all languages.

5.2 Old Japanese

Watanabe (2002), basing his analysis on descriptive work by Nomura (1993), argues that the Old Japanese of the eighth century had overt *wh*-movement. The data are drawn from *Man'yoshu*, an anthology of poems compiled in the eighth century. Nomura observes that in Old Japanese, the *wh*-phrase tends to occur on the left periphery of the clause—crucially, to the left of the subject phrase. The following example is taken from Watanabe 2002:182:

(1) Kado tate-te   to-mo   sashi-taru-wo *izuku-yu-ka*
    gate close-CONJ door-also shut-PAST-ACC where-through-KA
    imo-ga   iriki-te   yume-ni   mie-tsuru? (3117)
    wife-NOM enter-CONJ dream-LOC appear-PERF
    'From where did my wife come and appear in my dream, despite the fact that I closed the gate and shut the door?'

In this example, the object *wh*-phrase *izuku-yu-ka* 'where-through-KA' occurs to the left of the subject 'wife'. What is of particular interest is that beginning in the ninth century, movement of *ka*-marked phrases began to be lost. Apparently, what triggered this loss was separation of *ka* from the *wh*-phrase. In Isobe's (1990) study of *wh*-questions in the *Tale of Genji*, a psychological novel written by Lady Murasaki Shikibu in the tenth century, roughly one-third of the examples have *ka* on the *wh*-phrase, whereas in another third, the *wh*-phrase occurs by itself and *ka* appears toward the end of the sentence, just as it does in modern Japanese. The remaining third of the examples are similar to those with clause-final *ka*, except that the particle that occurs at the end is a different focus particle, *zo*, as in (2) (Watanabe 2002:187).

(2) Kono nisi-naru ie-ha   *nani-bito*-no   sumu-zo?
      this   west-be   house-TOP what-person-NOM live-Q
      'What person lives in this house to the west?'

In Watanabe's (2002) study, we observe Japanese changing from a *wh*-movement language to a *wh*-in-situ one. It is clear from the details of this change that the trigger is the status of the focus particle. During the movement stage of the language, a focus particle such as *ka* attached to the *wh*-phrase or to any focused phrase. With the change in the language that led to *ka* (or *zo*) appearing at question (or focus) C, the *wh*-phrase and other focus phrases stopped moving. This historical change in one language embodies the essence of what constitutes *wh*-questions in general. This is the topic I turn to in the next section.

5.3   *Wh*-Questions Contain a Focus Probe

Returning to *wh*-questions across languages, recall that one problem I raised in section 5.1 is that the Q feature on the question C is not uninterpretable, so it cannot probe for a feature contained in a *wh*-phrase, which would be its goal. Yet we know that some sort of Agree relation holds between the Q feature and a *wh*-phrase. We can see this, for example, from the fact that multiple-*wh* constructions exhibit superiority effects. What enables this Agree relation to obtain in a *wh*-question? Old Japanese provides an obvious clue: focus. Limiting our discussion to *ka*, the crucial factor is the location of the focus particle *ka*. If it attaches to a *wh*-phrase, the *wh*-phrase moves, but if it occurs on the question C, the *wh*-phrase does not move. Let us suppose the following characterization of *wh*-questions:

(3) Wh-*questions*
      A focus probe merges on the question C. It enters into Agree with
      the focus feature of the closest *wh*-phrase.

Recall from chapter 3 that the "focus probe" is in fact −focus, which, by itself, is topic, but when it enters into Agree with a focus phrase, it is valued as +focus. For simplicity, though, I will refer to the probe as *focus probe*. The idea in (3) is that the Q feature, like the ϕ-probe, needs a mechanism for seeking its goal. We saw that the ϕ-probe typically depends on Case, although we also saw in Kinande and Kilega that the topic probe or focus probe can play this role. Viewed in this way, *wh*-questions are similar to focus constructions, the one difference being that *wh*-questions have a Q feature on C.

(4)

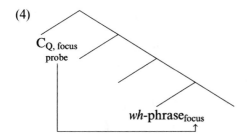

The Agree relation establishes a functional relation between the C head and the *wh*-phrase, in turn allowing the Q feature on C to establish an operator-variable relation with the *wh*-phrase. This is similar to how the topic feature "helps" the φ-probe at α to attain valuation in Kinande. An advantage to this way of viewing the relationship that the Q feature establishes with the *wh*-phrase is that this makes it possible for the Q feature to enter into multiple agreements that lead to multiple-*wh* questions. The focus probe may enter into agreement with however many *wh*-phrases exist, and with each instance of agreement, the Q feature is marked as being linked to the particular *wh*-phrase.

Three additional points are relevant. First, the relation that is established between the Q feature and the *wh*-phrase via the focus probe is retained beyond narrow syntax, as is necessary for semantic interpretation. Although the focus probe on C is erased in the transfer to semantic interpretation, Q is not erased because it is an interpretable feature. In this way, it is possible for Q to enter into Agree with multiple *wh*-phrases, the relations made possible via multiple agreement by a single focus probe. The focus probe is ultimately erased, but all of the relations that Q has established with *wh*-phrases are retained for semantic interpretation thanks to the interpretable nature of Q.

Second, why does focus play this role of establishing a functional relation between the question C and the *wh*-phrase? There are two reasons. First, as we have seen in the discussions up to now, focus (and topic) is a probe that is always potentially available along with the φ-probe. Second, focus and questions share the semantics of alternatives (Beck and Rullmann 1998, Hamblin 1973, Hagstrom 1998, Karttunen 1977, Kratzer and Shimoyama 2002, Ramchand 1997, Rooth 1992, 1996). In fact, if we excluded the Q feature of questions, questions and focus would be very similar in their semantic representation, although not necessarily identical (see Beck 2006).

Third, recall from the discussion of *pro*-drop that narrow syntax has two ways of attaining a probe-goal union (PGU). One is to move an XP "goal" to the label of the head that contains the φ-probe (Spec-head relation), and the other is to move an agreement head "goal" to the φ-probe (head movement). The historical change in Japanese *wh*-questions represents a change from one (Spec-head) to the other (head movement). The general pattern here is what Cheng (1991) calls "clause-typing" of questions. A *wh*-question is typed as such by either moving a *wh*-phrase to Spec,CP or inserting a question particle in lieu of *wh*-phrase movement. In Miyagawa 2001, I argued that this clause-typing of questions parallels the phenomenon that Alexiadou and Anagnostopoulou (1998) have identified for the EPP at T: either move the goal to Spec,TP or move the rich verbal morphology to T, a point originally due to Hagstrom (1998) (see also Landau 2007).

The proposed analysis also explains an otherwise mysterious fact about *wh*-questions and focus. In some languages (e.g., Old Japanese, Sinhala; see Kishimoto 2005), the same verbal inflection agrees with a *wh*-phrase or a focus phrase. In Old Japanese, the verb inflected for a variety of forms; two main forms were *conclusive* and *attributive*. For the most part, conclusive forms occurred in the matrix clause, and attributive forms in the subordinate clause.

(5) a. Sakana-o tabu.   (conclusive)
      fish-ACC   eat
      '(I/She/They/etc.) eat fish.'
   b. taburu sakana   (attributive)
      eat   fish
      'the fish that (I/she/they/etc.) eat'

The attributive form occurs unexpectedly in the matrix clause when there is a focus particle. I demonstrate this for the three focus particles *ya*, *zo*, and *ka*. (Examples (6a–c) are from Sansom 1928, and (6d) is from *Kokinshuu*.)

(6) a. Isi-wa   kawa-ni otu.   (conclusive)
      rock-TOP river-in fall
      'Rocks fall into the river.'
   b. Isi *zo* kawa-ni *oturu*.   (attributive)
   c. Isi *ya* kawa-ni *oturu*.   (attributive)
   d. Ikito si ikeru mono, izure *ka*   uta-o   (attributive)
      all-the-living things which KAKARI poem-ACC
      yomazarikeru.
      compose.NEG.E(ATTRIB)
      'Every living creature sings.'

As we can see, in the presence of *zo, ya,* or *ka,* the verb must be in the attributive form, a form of agreement with the focus particle. This construction is called *kakarimusubi.* Note that the same "focus agreement" occurs in *wh*-questions.

(7) Ikani motenai-tamahan-to suru ni-ka?
    how   treat.give-HON.V-C   do   LOC-KA
    'How is he going to treat me?'

The verb here is inflected for attributive, not conclusive.

For a typical *wh*-movement language such as English, the analysis proposed here would identify focus on *wh*-phrases. Because there is no focus particle that can split from the *wh*-phrase, the *wh*-phrase itself must move to the specifier of the focus probe head to value the focus probe. This is essentially the analysis of Watanabe (1992) (although he proposes that what moves is an empty *wh*-operator) and, of course, Hagstrom (1998) (although in his view the question particle *ka* is an existential quantifier, not focus). Also, Cable (2007) presents an extensive analysis of *wh*-questions based on Tlingit, which has both a *wh*-phrase and a question particle, similar to Japanese and Sinhala. His analysis independently develops many ideas that are similar to those in this chapter, particularly the role of focus in *wh*-questions and the need for the Q feature (which he calls "interrogative") to depend on a probe for establishing a link with a variable (in his case, a choice function).[2]

To summarize, the semantics of *wh*-questions contain a question (or existential) operator and a variable. Because the Q feature on C, which is the operator, is fully interpretable, it cannot probe for the relevant feature on the *wh*-phrase in order to enter into an Agree relation with it. A focus probe (−focus valued as +focus) is merged on the same C as the Q feature, and it functions as the probe to link the C head with the *wh*-phrase, by entering into an Agree relation with the focus feature on the *wh*-phrase.

5.4 Intervention Effects

In a variety of languages, certain items (called *intervenors*) cause ungrammaticality if one of them occurs between a *wh*-phrase in situ and the C at which the *wh*-phrase takes scope. Example (8b) shows a typical intervention effect in German.

(8) a.   Was glaubt Hans, *wen*   Karl gesehen hat?
         what believes Hans whom Karl seen   has
         'Who does Hans believe that Karl saw?'

b. *Was glaubt niemand, *wen*   Karl gesehen hat?
what believes nobody   whom Karl seen   has
'Who does nobody believe that Karl saw?'

In this *wh*-question, the "content" *wh*-phrase is *wen* 'whom'; it is this *wh*-phrase that must take matrix scope semantically. However, in this particular case, what occurs in the matrix Spec,CP is *was*, which in its normal usage means 'what' but here is a placeholder equivalent to an expletive (see McDaniel 1989). The problem arises with the occurrence of the negative universal expression *niemand* 'nobody' as shown in (8b), which somehow blocks the "real" *wh*-phrase *wen* 'whom' from taking scope at the matrix C. If we replace *niemand* with an R-expression, as in (8a), the example is grammatical (Beck 1996, Rizzi 1992), which suggests that some lexical property of *niemand* not shared by R-expressions induces intervention. The standard view of intervention is that it is caused by a scope-bearing item. It is, therefore, an effect induced by a quantificational expression. This is the view found in Hoji 1985, which is the first systematic study of intervention. Other studies adopting this view include Beck 1995, 1996, Beck and Kim 1997, Chang 1997, Hagstrom 1998, Miyagawa 1998, Pesetsky 2000, Rizzi 1992, Takahashi 1990, and Tanaka 1997.

More recently, however, a different view has emerged that points to focus as the source of intervention effects (Beck 2006, Kim 2002, 2006). Kim (2002), who first proposed this, observes that not all quantifiers induce an intervention effect (see Beck and Kim 1997) and that those that do are associated with focus. Following Kim's work, Beck (2006) makes a similar observation: crosslinguistically, it is focus expressions such as the 'only' phrase that induce the strongest intervention effects. In this section, I will argue for this focus-based approach to intervention. I will give a syntactic argument to support the view that only focused phrases in Japanese function as intervenors. This provides further evidence that what I have called focus in Japanese, *ka*, is in fact a bearer of focus.

The focused phrases in Japanese relevant to intervention are morphologically transparent; they are existential expressions with the particle *ka* (e.g., *dare-ka* 'someone') (Miyagawa 1998) and universal expressions with the universal particle *mo* (e.g., *dare-mo* 'everyone') (Hagstrom 1998, Shimoyama 2001, 2006). This demonstrates that along with the semantic function of indicating existence (*ka*) or universality (*mo*), these particles show that the phrase they attach to is associated with focus. The idea that focus induces intervention receives clear support when we compare, for example, two universal expressions, one with *mo* and the other without: only the expression with *mo* induces intervention. This shows that intervention is not quantificational in nature; rather, it indicates focus. Relevant examples will follow shortly.

Beck (2006) provides a formal semantic account of Kim's original "focus" insight. I will adopt the core of their insight—that intervention is a matter of focus. I will capture this within a focus-probe approach to *wh*-questions. After reviewing the intervention data in Japanese, I will show that the syntactic approach that Kim (2006) proposes follows straightforwardly from the focus-probe approach.

5.4.1 Quantifier-Induced Barrier

Abstracting away from the details of their analyses, the linguists adopting the standard view of intervention effects see an intervenor as blocking movement of the *wh*-expression, as the German example (8b) illustrates. Under this analysis, in (8b), *wen* 'whom' must move to the matrix Spec,CP for proper interpretation of the *wh*-question, but the intervenor, *niemand* 'nobody', somehow blocks this movement. The following is an example from Japanese (Hoji (1985) first noted this type of example):[3]

(9) *Daremo-ga   nani-o   katta   no?
    everyone-NOM what-ACC bought Q
    'What did everyone buy?'

Here the intervenor is the quantifier *daremo* 'everyone', which is composed of the indeterminate pronoun/*wh*-phrase *dare* 'who' and the particle *mo*, which creates universal expressions when combined with an indeterminate pronoun. In both German and Japanese, the ostensible *wh*-movement that is blocked by an intervenor would be covert movement (see Huang 1982). Does an intervenor block overt movement? Example (10) shows that the answer is no, given that overt scrambling of the *wh*-phrase over the universal quantifier leads to a grammatical question (Hoji 1985).

(10) Nani-o$_i$ daremo-ga t_i katta   no?
     what-ACC everyone-NOM   bought Q
     'What did everyone buy?'

The same covert/overt difference emerges in the following French examples from Chang 1997:

(11) a. *?Jean ne   mange pas quoi?
            Jean NEG eat   NEG what
     b.   Que ne   mange-t-il pas?
          what NEG eat-he   NEG
          'What doesn't Jean eat?'

In (11a), the *wh*-phrase presumably stays in situ, a type of construction allowed in the root clause in French. The intervenor *ne* (*pas*) blocks covert raising of *quoi* to Spec,CP. In (11b), the overt movement of *que* to Spec,CP is not blocked by the negative intervenor.

What are the items in a language that induce an intervention effect? Hoji (1985) explicitly identifies quantifiers as blocking covert *wh*-movement. He notes that if a quantifier c-commands a *wh*-phrase, and the quantifier itself is c-commanded by the C associated with the question force, the sentence is ungrammatical because the *wh*-phrase must raise covertly over the quantifier.

(12) *[... [$_{C[+Q]}$ [$_{TP}$ ... quantifier ... *wh*-phrase ...]]]

Hoji reduces this ungrammaticality to the language-specific property of quantifier scope rigidity (Kuroda 1971)—namely, the property that only surface scope is permitted at LF for scope-bearing items including *wh*-phrases. In (12), the quantifier undergoes Quantifier Raising (QR) to TP, but the *wh*-phrase must raise to Spec,CP, thereby reversing the surface c-command relation in violation of scope rigidity.

Beck (1996) formalizes the intervention effect as follows (see also Beck and Kim 1997):

(13) *Quantifier-induced barrier (QUIB)*
      The first node that dominates a quantifier, its restriction, and its nuclear scope is a quantifier-induced barrier.

(14) *

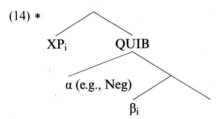

In (14), α is a quantifier, and the node that immediately dominates it is a QUIB that blocks movement of the XP from the position of β. Beck further states that the type of chain susceptible to a QUIB is created at LF, by covert movement. This presumably is because, in this type of approach, scope-taking quantifiers induce the QUIB effect, and scope-taking is typically viewed as an LF phenomenon (e.g., QR). By specifying that only covert movement is blocked by a QUIB, this approach takes account of the fact that a QUIB does not block overt movement of a *wh*-phrase. I should note, however, that in the end, we are not certain why this overt/covert distinction exists.

Some of the analyses mentioned above address the overt/covert issue by assuming a neutral stance on whether the *wh*-movement is overt or covert. Rizzi (1992) analyzes the German examples in (8) as involving the movement of a piece of the "real" *wh*-phrase, possibly the *wh*-operator portion that is not pronounced, as in Watanabe 1992. Because the *wh*-operator portion is just a piece of the argument *wh*-phrase *wen* 'whom', this movement does not count as movement of an argument; hence, the movement is subject to the Empty Category Principle, a version of which is Rizzi's (1990) Relativized Minimality. Because there is a quantifier in (8b), that quantifier is closer to the *wh*-phrase than C, which causes a Minimality violation. Taking a similar tack, Pesetsky (2000) assumes that what moves in the *wh*-in-situ construction is the *wh*-feature; what remains is the semantic restriction of the *wh*-phrase. He proposes the following constraint to account for the intervention effect (Pesetsky 2000:67):[4]

(15) *Intervention effect (universal characterization)*
A semantic restriction on a quantifier (including *wh*) may not be separated from that quantifier by a scope-bearing element.

Both Rizzi's and Pesetsky's accounts depend on the intervenor being a quantifier. Hagstrom's (1998) analysis is also developed along these lines, except that in his case what moves in *wh*-in-situ constructions is the question particle. As noted earlier, Cheng (1991) observes that languages often have a way to overtly mark a *wh*-question, either by moving the *wh*-phrase to the head of the sentence or, if the *wh*-phrase does not move, by marking the construction with a question particle. Hagstrom (1998) argues that these two movements are equivalent; in both cases, something moves to C, and it is the question particle that is subject to intervention effects (see his work for details)—again, assuming that the intervenor is a quantifier.

5.4.2 An Alternative View of Intervention

In discussing her own work with Beck (Beck and Kim 1997), Kim (2002) argues that the earlier work has a serious flaw—namely, not all quantifiers induce an intervention effect (Beck and Kim 1997:369–372). Although negative polarity items (NPIs) and a handful of other scope-bearing elements are intervenors, the following quantificational expressions do not induce intervention in Korean: *taepupun-ui N* 'most N', *hangsang* 'always', and *chachu* 'often'.[5] These happen not to be associated with focus, and this leads Kim to the focus-based analysis of intervention.

In the remainder of this chapter, I argue that the focus approach to intervention is correct and that it gives evidence that there is focus in *wh*-questions that is identical to the focus in focused expressions such as *mo* and *ka* phrases.

5.4.2.1 Focus Barriers   To substantiate the focus approach to intervention, let us look at some data from Japanese. The intervenors in Japanese are morphologically transparent: they include either the existential particle *ka* (Miyagawa 1998) or the universal particle *mo* (Hagstrom 1998). The following is, I believe, an exhaustive, or close to exhaustive, set of intervenors in Japanese:

(16) *With universal* mo
      Universal quantifier (Hoji 1985)
      ?*Dare*mo*-ga   nani-o   katta   no?
      everyone-NOM what-ACC bought Q
      'Everyone bought what?'

(17) *With* ka
      a. *NPI* sika-nai *'only'* (Takahashi 1990)[6]
         *Taroo-si*ka* nani-o   kawa-nakat-ta no?
         Taro-only what-ACC buy-NEG-PAST Q
         'What did only Taro buy?'
      b. *Existential quantifier* (Hoji 1985)
         ??Dare*ka*-ga   nani-o   katta   no?
         someone-NOM what-ACC bought Q
         'Someone bought what?'

The effect of any of these intervenors can be overcome by overtly moving the *wh*-phrase over it. I demonstrate this for the NPI *sika-nai* 'only' in (18).

(18) *NPI* sika-nai *'only'*
      Nani-o$_i$ Taroo-si*ka* t_i kawa-nakat-ta no?
      what-ACC Taro-only   buy-NEG-PAST Q
      'What did only Taro buy?'

5.4.2.2 *Mo* and *Ka* Phrases Are Focus   We have already seen that *mo* phrases are associated with focus. As noted in chapter 1, the *mo* expression carries focus stress. Note the minimal pair in (19).

(19) a. Taroo-wa HON-o   katta.
         Taro-TOP book-ACC bought
         'Taro bought a book.'

    b. TAROO-*mo* hon-o   katta.
       Taro-also   book-ACC bought
       'Taro also bought a book.'

In (19a), which has no special focused element, the object receives the default prominence. In (19b), the *mo* subject phrase attracts this prominence, showing that it carries focus. Moreover, as Hasegawa (1991, 1994) points out, when occurring with sentential negation, the *mo* phrase is interpreted outside the scope of negation.

(20) a. John-mo ko-nakat-ta.
       John-also come-NEG-PAST
       'John (in addition to someone else) did not come.'
    b. John-ga   hon-mo   kaw-anakat-ta.
       John-NOM book-also buy-NEG-PAST
       'A book is one of things that John did not buy.'

Example (20a) has only the interpretation that there is at least one person who did not come besides John. It does not mean that someone came, but John didn't come as well, which would be the interpretation if the *mo* phrase were inside the negative scope.[7] Likewise, (20b) means only that John did not buy something besides a book; it does not mean that John bought something but not also a book. I have argued that this phenomenon whereby the *mo* phrase takes scope outside the sentential negation of its clause indicates that movement has occurred (see Hasegawa 2005). Movement, in turn, shows that there is a probe; and in the case of *mo*, the probe agrees with the focus feature on the *mo* phrase.

5.4.2.3 Intervenors Are Focused Phrases If we apply the "focus" test to the intervenors exemplified in (16) and (17), we see that each one has the property Hasegawa (1991, 1994) identified—namely, it is interpreted outside the scope of negation (Hasegawa 1991 notes this for *ka* as well as *mo*).

(21) *With universal* mo
    a. *Universal quantifier* (Hoji 1985)
       Taroo-ga daremo-o   mi-na-akat-ta.
       Taro-NOM everyone-ACC see-NEG-PAST
       'Taro did not see everyone.'
       *not > everyone, everyone > not
    b. *'Almost every'* (Miyagawa 1998)
       Taroo-ga hotondo daremo-o   mi-nakat-ta.
       Taro-NOM almost   everyone-ACC see-NEG-PAST

'Taro did not see almost everyone.'
*not > almost every, almost every > not
  c. *'Also'*
Taroo-ga hon-mo kaw-anakat-ta.
Taro-NOM book-too buy-NEG-PAST
'Taro did not also buy a book.'
*not > also, also > not

(22) *With* ka
  a. *NPI* sika-nai *'only'* (Takahashi 1990)
  Not applicable because this is an NPI.
  b. *Existential quantifier* (Hoji 1985)
  Taroo-ga dare*ka*-o   mi-nakat-ta.
  Taro-NOM someone-ACC see-NEG-PAST
  'Taro did not see someone.'
  *not > someone, someone > not
  c. *Disjunction* ka (Hoji 1985)
  Taroo-ga [John-*ka* Mary]-o   mi-nakat-ta.
  Taro-NOM John-or Mary-ACC see-NEG-PAST
  'Taro did not see John or Mary.'
  or > not, *not > or

As shown, all *mo* and *ka* phrases are focused and enter into Agree with the focus probe on T, making it mandatory for them to move to Spec,TP and be interpreted outside sentential negation. This explains why, in (22c), disjunction 'or' in Japanese does not have the 'universal' reading associated with *or* in English (*Taro didn't see John or Mary*). Although the object disjunctive phrase in English may stay in object position, where it is in the scope of negation that leads to the universal interpretation of *or*, in Japanese, the focus probe that enters into Agree with focus of the disjunction phrase with *ka* 'or' forces this phrase to raise to Spec,TP and outside the scope of negation, thus depriving it of the universal reading.[8]

5.4.2.4 Nonfocused Quantifiers Are Not Intervenors We have seen that universal expressions formed with *mo* and existential expressions formed with *ka* are focused expressions that raise to Spec,TP. Following Kim (2002, 2006) and Beck (2006), I assume that it is this focus property, and not the quantificational nature of these expressions, that makes them intervenors. One clear piece of evidence for this is found with expressions that are very close in meaning to the intervenors. For example, the word *minna* 'all/everyone' has a meaning similar to that of the intervenor *daremo* 'everyone', yet it does not induce an intervention effect (Hoji 1985).

(23) Minna-ga   nani-o   katta no?
     all/everyone-NOM what-ACC bought Q
     'What did all/everyone buy?'

Minna is not formed with one of the "focus" particles (e.g., *mo*), so it is not lexically marked for focus.[9] One possible counterargument is that *minna* in (23) has the group reading common to the word *all*, hence it is not behaving like a quantifier, so (23) really doesn't tell us that it is focus, not quantification, that is relevant for intervention. We can respond to this with (24), in which *minna* clearly has distributional—hence quantificational—meaning.

(24) Minna-ga   sorezore nani-o   katta no?
     everyone-NOM each   what-ACC bought Q
     'What did everyone each buy?'

This question is most naturally interpreted as a pair-list question, which signifies that 'what' distributes over the members of the set designated by *minna sorezore* 'everyone each'. This indicates that *minna* functions as a quantifier. Even so, *minna* does not induce an intervention effect.[10]

Kim (2002) (see also Beck and Kim 1997) points out that the Korean expressions *taepupun-ui N* 'most N', *chachu* 'often', and *hangsang* 'always' are not intervenors despite their quantificational nature. In Japanese, too, these do not induce an intervention effect.

(25) a. Hotondo-no hito-ga   nani-o   katta no?
        most-GEN people-NOM what-ACC bought Q
        'What did most people buy?'
     b. Hanako-ga yoku nani-o   asa   taberu no?
        Hanako-NOM often what-ACC morning eat   Q
        'What does Hanako often eat in the morning?'
     c. Taroo-ga itu-mo nani-o   asa   taberu no?
        Taro-NOM always what-ACC morning eat   Q
        'What does Taro always eat in the morning?'

Neither *hotondo-no N* 'most N' nor *yoku* 'often' is a focused expression, in that neither contains a particle equivalent to *mo* or *ka*. What is surprising is *itu-mo* 'always', which is composed of the indeterminate pronoun *itu* 'when' and the universal particle *mo*. This has the same morphology as intervenors such as *dare-mo* 'everyone', yet it apparently does not induce an intervention effect. I do not know why *itu-mo* is able to be free of focus, but the facts are clear.

There are two differences, very much related, between *itu-mo* 'always' and an intervenor like *dare-mo* 'everyone'. First, unlike *dare-mo*, *itu-mo* does not attract stress in sentences with neutral prosody. This means that focus does not arise every time *mo* appears.

(26) Taroo-ga itu-mo PIZA-o   taberu.
     Taro-NOM always pizza-ACC eat
     'Taro always eats pizza.'

This suggests that *itu-mo* 'always' is not inherently focused. This in turn predicts that it is not the goal of a focus probe. Example (27) shows that this prediction is borne out.

(27) Taroo-ga itu-mo piza-o   tabe-nai.
     Taro-NOM always pizza-ACC eat-NEG
     'Taro does not always eat pizza.'
     not > always, always > not

As shown, *itu-mo* can be interpreted inside the scope of local sentential negation ('not > always'), something that is difficult, if not impossible, with *dare-mo* 'everyone'. This shows that *itu-mo* may stay in situ in a position under Spec,TP. For the other reading, 'always > not', one could imagine that *itu-mo* undergoes QR, which it is free to do because it does not enter into an Agree relation with a focus probe.

5.4.3 Intervention as a Relativized Minimality Violation

In this section, I analyze intervention effects as being induced by focus. Drawing on data from Korean and Hindi (see Lahiri 1998 for Hindi), Kim (2002) argues that the true source of intervention effects is focus. Later (Kim 2006), she provides a syntactic approach to intervention by incorporating into her analysis the notions of interpretable and uninterpretable features.

(28) *$[_{CP}$ $C_{[iQ, iF]}$ $[\ldots Foc_{[iF]} \ldots [\ldots [wh_{[uQ, uF]} \ldots]]]]$
       └─────────────────────────────────┘

The question C contains the interpretable Q and interpretable focus features, and they must be linked together to their uninterpretable counterparts contained in a *wh*-phrase. The problem with (28) is that it violates Relativized Minimality: the focus feature on C finds as its closest counterpart the interpretable focus feature on the focus expression Foc instead of on the *wh*-phrase.[11]

We can improve on Kim's Relativized Minimality approach by simplifying the features that are involved, and by taking into account what we found with the focused *ka* and *mo* phrases: that they enter into an Agree relation with a focus probe. Let us suppose that the focus feature on the focused phrase—the intervenor—and the focus feature on the *wh*-phrase are identical, contrary to Kim's analysis in (28). This makes intuitive the fact that they interact in a way that induces a Relativized Minimality violation under certain structural conditions. Also, each focus feature in the structure requires a focus probe to enter into an Agree relation. I propose (29) as the initial structure that leads to intervention. Following Hagstrom (1998), I will assume that the question particle *ka* is merged next to the *wh*-phrase. In giving the structure, I will arbitrarily use the head-initial representation.

(29) $C_{Q, \text{ focus probe, focus probe}}$ $[\dots T \dots XP_{\text{focus}} \dots wh\text{-phrase-}ka_{\text{focus}}]$

There are two focus probes on C: one for the focus phrase, the other for the *wh*-phrase. They enter into Agree with the respective phrases that carry focus.

(30) $C_{Q, \text{ focus probe, focus probe}}$ $[\dots T \dots XP_{\text{focus}} \dots wh\text{-phrase-}ka_{\text{focus}} \dots]$

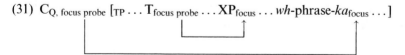

Presumably, the first Agree relation is with the focus XP, and the second is with the focus feature on the *wh*-phrase. Conceivably, the second Agree relation may be considered to be impossible owing to a defective intervention effect, but let us keep to the simplest assumption, namely, that once the first Agree relation is established, the focus feature on the XP is neutralized for the purposes of Agree, and the second Agree relation can then establish itself across the focus XP. At this point, one of the focus probes is inherited by T.

(31) $C_{Q, \text{ focus probe}}$ $[_{\text{TP}} \dots T_{\text{focus probe}} \dots XP_{\text{focus}} \dots wh\text{-phrase-}ka_{\text{focus}} \dots]$

At this point, the goal must move to the probe for PGU. The focus XP encounters no problem; it moves to Spec,TP. But a problem does arise for the *wh*-phrase. The focus particle *ka*, merged by the *wh*-phrase, must move to $C_{Q, \text{ focus probe}}$, but the closest focus probe is the focus probe on T. This focus probe on T blocks *ka* from moving all the way to C, thereby prohibiting the functional relation between the focus probe on C and the focus feature on the *wh*-phrase that is needed to attain PGU.[12] In contrast, if the *wh*-phrase with *ka* scrambles above the TP, the intervention is avoided. I presume that this phrase lands in αP.

(32) $C_{Q, \text{ focus probe}}$ [$_{αP}$ *wh*-phrase-*ka*$_{\text{focus}}$ [$_{TP}$ ... T$_{\text{focus probe}}$ ... XP$_{\text{focus}}$ ...]]

From this position, *ka* is able to move to C and implement a PGU with the appropriate focus probe at C.

5.5 Summary

In this chapter, I argued that *wh*-questions contain a focus probe (−focus that is valued as +focus) at C that agrees with the focus feature on the *wh*-phrase. This makes it possible for the Q feature at C to enter into a relation with the *wh*-feature on the *wh*-phrase. The focus probe is necessary for Q to acquire this relation because Q, being an interpretable feature, cannot probe for a goal on its own. The focus probe can enter into an agreement relation with one or more *wh*-phrases. In each case, Q, which is not a probe, benefits by having a true probe (focus) create the needed relation. Even after the focus probe is erased, Q retains its relation to the *wh*-phrase and this makes the appropriate semantic interpretation possible. Q is retained beyond narrow syntax because of its interpretable nature. The movement of the *wh*-phrase is due to the focus portion of the construction, which requires PGU to take place. Likewise, in the *wh*-in-situ language Japanese, movement takes place, but what moves is the minimal focus element, *ka*. We saw that historically, in terms of *wh*-questions, Japanese changed from a *wh*-phrase movement language to the current "particle" movement (*wh*-in-situ) language. Finally, in an extensive look at intervention effects, I showed that the recent focus-based approach to intervention provides another argument for the occurrence of the focus probe in *wh*-questions.

6   Concluding Remarks

I set out to try to provide plausible answers to the questions "Why is there agreement in human language?" and "Why is there movement?" If any of what I argued for is on the right track, the real answer, setting aside the intricacies of how agreement and movement work in narrow syntax, is that their interaction imbues language with the enormous expressiveness that makes it what it is. Without them, we humans would be abysmally handicapped in expressing our thoughts. Topic-comment (or theme-rheme), subject of a clause, focus, content questions, and other notions would be absent from our cognitive life as far as language is concerned.

For this system to work properly, all the pieces must fit together perfectly; one piece missing, and the entire system falls flat. The sparseness I tried to attain—and I'm sure there are a number of components that can be simplified further with deeper understanding—led to some open and critical questions that I must leave for future study. But my hope is that where I was able to provide answers, those answers proved to be deeper and more interesting because I attempted to capture them with as few assumptions as possible.

Notes

Preface

1. Relational Grammar (RG) also has a linearization component, although it is nowhere as extensively developed or formalized as the linearization component in Kayne's work. Blake (1990) describes the RG linearization as follows, basing his characterization in part on Perlmutter's comments in the afterword to Perlmutter and Postal 1983. The need for linearization arises because "[r]elational networks are unordered representations" (Blake 1990:20), all relations being strictly hierarchical, and linearization occurs as the last step in the derivation of a sentence.

Chapter 1

1. Fassi Fehri (1993:34–38) provides a brief overview of asymmetries found in a number of languages. Thanks to Omer Preminger for pointing me to this work.

2. In these dialects, tonic pronouns and full NPs in preverbal position are accompanied by a subject clitic that also agrees with the subject. The occurrence of this clitic has no bearing on my argument that movement is correlated with full agreement. See Brandi and Cordin 1989 for discussion of subject clitics in these dialects.

3. As mentioned, a reasonable way to view (7a) (*There appears to be a man in the garden*) is that nothing appears in the embedded Spec,TP, and nothing is "raised," but instead, the expletive is inserted directly into Spec,TP of the root clause. This would mean that in the following example, where the subject *Mary* clearly has raised from the embedded clause, it did not go through Spec,TP:

(i) Mary$_i$ seems to him to like herself$_i$ (*her$_i$).

Presumably, *Mary* raises directly from the lower Spec,vP to the matrix Spec,TP. Thanks to Noam Chomsky for bringing examples like these to my attention.

4. As Noam Chomsky (pers. comm.) has noted, there are questions about the validity of structure preservation, as in the case of the structure that arises from object shift or from stacking of *wh*-phrases found in some languages (e.g., Richards

2001). If these turn out to be genuine exceptions to structure preservation, we will need to qualify the idea that Merge, external and internal, is a unified operation. I will leave this issue open.

5. There is another, equally important function of agreement. As I explain later in this chapter, probes ("uninterpretable features") are initially merged only on phase heads such as C and v (Chomsky 2005, 2007, 2008). In essence, therefore, agreement, and specifically probes, define phases, which are the domains of computation in narrow syntax. A particularly significant point is that agreement appears to keep phases as small as possible (Chomsky 2007), possibly for computational efficiency and simplicity. I will not discuss this function of agreement in this monograph, although it is important to note that it complements what I will discuss, and does not in any way contradict it.

6. A proposal consonant with mine is Chung's (1998) notion of associate relation. Associate relations are very close to—possibly the same as—the functional relations that I propose. The associate relation is basically a relation that holds between a functional head and its specifier or a projection of the functional head (Chung 1998:179). Chung describes this relation of a nominal to a functional head as critical to agreement, a proposal I concur with. Like the functional relation, the associate relation establishes a relation between a nominal (mostly) and a functional head, and it "contributes significantly to syntactic licensing" (Chung 1998:5). I take this notion of syntactic licensing to be equivalent to (possibly identical with) the notion of functional relation, whereby a nominal is licensed within the larger syntactic-expression clause in which it occurs. Although Chung does not give a clear motivation for the associate relation, if the proposal in this monograph is in any way on the right track, the evidence I present for the existence of agreement will also be evidence for the associate relation.

7. A reviewer notes that agreement sometimes shows up in nominal clauses, and it is not always certain whether this agreement involves the D head. I will assume that such agreement always involves the D head or some other functional relation, but I will not attempt to defend this assumption here.

8. A number of linguists have pointed out to me that the indeterminate pronoun is associated with two distinct prominence patterns, the "normal" pattern where the first mora in *dare* 'who' receives prominence (*DAre*) and a second pattern where no prominence is associated with this word. The first pattern leads to the ungrammatical judgment of (20) noted by Kishimoto (2001), but the second pattern improves the sentence. If this is indeed the case, then we can surmise that the first pattern associates focus with the indeterminate pronoun, forcing it to raise to Spec,TP, but the second pattern does not, allowing the indeterminate pronoun to stay in situ within the scope of *mo*. This would be a further confirmation that focus forces movement. Throughout this monograph, I will use the first pattern.

9. In other work, Chomsky (2007), adopting a suggestion by Marc Richards, argues that the need for inheritance arises from the probe-goal system within the phase architecture of narrow syntax. The idea is that an uninterpretable feature (probe) must be erased before being transferred to semantic interpretation. In the probe-goal system, the goal values the probe, and it is assumed that, once valued,

the uninterpretable feature looks exactly like the interpretable feature of the goal. To ensure that the system can identify which features were formerly uninterpretable features, the probe and the goal must be in the same transfer (spell-out) domain. Because the complement of the phase head (e.g., TP, which is the complement of the phase head C) undergoes transfer, inheritance is needed to place the probe as well as the goal in the same transfer domain (e.g., TP). Since in later chapters I will generalize the probe-goal system for agreement not only at TP, but also at CP, I am unable to fully adopt the approach just described; instead, I will continue to make the earlier assumption that inheritance occurs to make A-chains available to language.

10. When the object becomes the agreed-with phrase, it moves from within VP to Spec,vP. I will give arguments showing why the object, being part of agreement, must move to Spec,vP. This will be one of the central themes of this monograph. On a phase-based approach to movement, this is not the only movement that occurs, however. The object presumably first moves from within VP to Spec,vP, the edge of the first phase. What drives this movement? It is clearly not triggered by agreement. Chomsky (2007) proposes that all heads may be associated with what he calls an edge feature that attracts an element to it, and that this edge feature is independent of any other feature such as agreement. I will not attempt to justify this proposal, but will simply assume it for these "intermediate" movements that set the stage for the kinds of movement I wish to deal with.

11. There are some potential problems with the idea that φ-probes require Case. For example, in Greek (Iatridou 1993), subject-verb agreement takes place in subjunctive as well as finite clauses, the former apparently without tense. There are a number of possible solutions for these problems, possibly along the lines of those proposed for Chinese in chapter 2 and Bantu in chapter 4. I will leave this open. See George and Kornfilt 1981 for similar issues related to Case and agreement.

Chapter 2

1. In some ways, this view recalls the model of movement found in the earliest minimalist literature (e.g., Chomsky 1993), where movement takes place to "check" a feature. As part of this checking process, the entire XP that contains the relevant feature is pied-piped, because phonology does not allow just the feature to raise. That is also true in the present proposal.

2. In indicating that movement has occurred in the examples, I will use the GB practice of marking the original position of the moved item with *t* (trace). Not only is this still the most widely used practice; it also stays neutral about the nature of the entity in this original position—a full copy or something reduced. In chapter 4, I will propose a way to predict the nature of the entity in the original position.

Also, I will use bar levels such as V, V′, and VP, strictly for expository purposes.

3. As a reviewer notes, whereas *the a book* is ungrammatical, Sabel's approach has to allow [*there a book*]. On Sabel's account, *the* and *there* are both D, so a way

must be found to block one from occurring with *a* (*the a) but not the other (*there a*). Moro's account is superior in this regard since it identifies the expletive as a predicate and not D.

4. I have focused on the *there* construction and have ignored the other expletive, *it*. I will simply mention that there is an analysis of expletive *it* that is similar to the analysis of *there* that I have described. The following is a typical expletive construction with *it* (Akmajian and Heny 1975:280).

(i) It is obvious that the world is round.

Stroik (1996) suggests that *it* in this construction begins in the Spec,CP of the embedded clause and raises to the matrix Spec,TP. One piece of evidence for this is the asymmetry shown in (ii) and (iii).

(ii) a. I just knew that Mary would fire John today.
     b. I just knew it that Mary would fire John today.

(iii) a. I just knew where Mary would fire John today.
      b. *I just knew it where Mary would fire John today.

The reason for the ungrammaticality of (iiib) is that *it* and *where* both occur in Spec,CP, violating the Doubly Filled Comp Filter; doubly filled Comp is not a problem in (iib) because *that* is a head. Although many details need to be filled in, this analysis of expletive *it* parallels the analysis given in the text for *there* in the sense that *it* is the goal with the interpretable feature and that it values the probe and moves to the probe under PGU.

5. The idea that a proxy for the goal meets the PGU requirement may also be applicable to the well-known *que/qui* facts in French (Rizzi 1990). The following examples are taken from Taraldsen 2002:29:

(i) Quel livre crois-tu   que/*qui les filles vont acheter?
    which book think-you that   the girls will buy
    'Which book do you think that the girls will buy?'

(ii) Quelles filles crois-tu   *que/qui vont acheter ce   livre-là?
     which   girls think-you that   will buy   that book-there
     'Which girls do you think will buy that book?'

Rizzi suggests that the *qui* form of the complementizer agrees with the subject *wh*-phrase and that this agreement licenses the movement of the subject *wh*-phrase into the lower Spec,CP.

   Taraldsen (2002) has argued that *qui* is *que* plus the expletive *i*.

(iii) quelles filles ... [CP que [IP *i* vont+I ...]]

The subject *wh*-phrase starts out lower in the structure, as in Italian (see Rizzi 1990, Taraldsen 2002). On this account, *i* is a proxy for the goal and, as such, is able to attain PGU with the embedded T's probe. This analysis brings the *que/qui* alternation into line with the resumptive/expletive construction in Danish and Swedish, overcoming a potential *that-t* violation. See Taraldsen 2002 for details.

6. The stipulation that when there is a complementizer, the subject *wh*-phrase is not allowed to move into the Spec,TP below the complementizer also can account

for typical cases of antiagreement (thanks to a reviewer for suggesting that I look at antiagreement in Berber). Berber has subject-verb agreement, with the agreeing inflection on the verb showing up as both pre-stem and post-stem (Ouhalla 1993, 2005). The following is a simple example. (Unless otherwise noted, the data are from Ouhalla 1993, 2005.)

(i) Lsa-nt   tifruxin ijllabn.
   wore-3F.PL girls   jellabas
   'The girls wore jellabas.'

As Ouhalla notes, when the subject is extracted in relative clause and cleft constructions, the agreement inflection cannot show up, resulting in what is commonly called antiagreement.

(ii) TAFRUXT ay sqad-n/*t-sqad   tabratt.
    girl   c send-PART/3F-send letter
    'It was the girl who sent the letter.'

(iii) SHEK   ay iuggur-n/*t-ggurt-t.
    you.M.SG c leave-PART/2M-leave-2M.SG
    'YOU are the one who left.'

Examples (iv)–(vi), taken from Elouazizi 2005:122–123, show the contrast between subject and object extractions, where subject extraction leads to antiagreement (AA) but object extraction does not.

(iv) Wh-*questions*
    a. Uw (g) y-wʃi-n/(*y-wʃa)   Iktab   (AA)
       who X PART-give.PERF-PART/(*3M.SG-give.PERF) book
       i Mena?
       to Mena
       'Who gave the book to Mena?'
    b. Min y-wʃa/(*y-wʃi-n)   Jamal   (no AA)
       what 3M.SG-give.PERF/(*PART-give.PERF-PART) Jamal
       i Mena?
       to Mena
       'What did Jamal give to Mena?'

(v) *Relative clauses*
    a. Y-ssqad   w-ar yaz   θabrat i Mena.   (no AA)
       3M.SG-send.PERF CS-man.M.SG letter   to Mena
       'The man sent the letter to Mena.'
    b. Zri-x   ar yaz   i (g)   (AA)
       see.PERF-1SG man.M.SG RM X
       y-ssqad-n/(*y-ssqad)   θabrat i Mena.
       PART-send.PERF-PART/(*3M.SG-send.PERF) letter   to Mena
       'I saw the man who sent the letter to Mena.'
    c. θabrat i (g) y-ssqad/(*y-ssqad-n)   (no AA)
       letter   RM X 3M.SG-send.PERF/(*PART-send.PERF-PART)
       w-ar yaz   i Mena θ-xʃʃ   d.
       CS-man.M.SG to Mena 3F.SG-arrive.PERF CL.dir
       'The letter which the man sent to Mena has arrived.'

(vi) *Cleft constructions*

    a. Y-ssqad   w-ar yaz   θabrat.   (no AA)
        3M.SG-send.PERF CS-man.M.SG letter
        'The man sent the/a letter.'

    b. (ð) ar yaz   i   (g) y-ssqad-n/(*y-ssqad)   (AA)
        COP man.M.SG CM X PART-send.PERF-PART/(*3M.SG-send.PERF)
        θabrat.
        letter
        'It is the man who sent the letter.'

    c. (T) θabrat i   (g) y-ssqad   w-ar yaz.   (no AA)
        COP letter CM X 3M.SG-send.PERF CS-man.M.SG
        'It is a letter that the man sent.'

Why is agreement suppressed when the subject, but not the object, *wh*-phrase is extracted to Spec,CP? I hypothesize that movement is triggered by the need to attain PGU. In the subject extraction cases, the subject *wh*-phrase has been extracted across a complementizer, and this complementizer, by stipulation, didn't allow the *wh*-phrase to move to Spec,TP below the complementizer. As a result, PGU is not attained at the point where this TP is transferred.

7. A reviewer notes that at least for languages such as Italian, the idea that Spec,TP is never filled has been disputed.

8. I thank Jim Huang and Dylan Tsai for assistance with this section. All mistakes are my responsibility.

9. For additional evidence that Chinese has tense, see Tsai, to appear. Tsai argues that, for tense, Chinese employs morphosyntactic measures instead of the morphological representation typically found in languages where tense is clearly marked. He calls this "tense anchoring." From this perspective, Chinese is a syntactic tense language, and the difference between English and Chinese lies in the way they realize the underlying event argument for tense operator binding— English by morphology and Chinese through syntax.

10. See Xu 1986 for a different approach to these examples, and for counterexamples.

11. Pan (2000) notes another possible issue regarding the blocking effect— namely, not all person conflicts lead to a blocking effect. If the local antecedent is third person, then a nonthird person in the higher clause can function as the antecedent.

(i) a. Wo$_i$ zhidao Lisi$_j$ bu xihuan ziji$_{?i/j}$.
       I   know Lisi not like   self
       'I knew that Lisi did not like me/himself.'

    b. Ni$_i$ xiang mei xiang guo Lisi$_j$ conglai jiu   mei xihuan guo ziji$_{?i/j}$?
       you think not think ASP Lisi never CONJ not like   ASP self
       'Have you ever thought about the idea that Lisi never liked you/himself?'

    c. Wo$_i$ yizhi yiwei Zhangsan$_j$ xihuan ziji$_{i/j}$, keshi wo cuo   le.
       I   so.far think Zhangsan like   self but I   wrong PRT
       'I always thought that Zhangsan liked me/himself, but I was wrong.'

In these examples, the lower subject is third person, and it does not block a first- or second-person subject in the higher clause from functioning as the antecedent. This is not at all inconsistent with what is known about person agreement. In Finnish, for example, which is a *pro*-drop language, first- and second-person agreements, but not third-person, sanction *pro*-drop (Holmberg 2005). Observing these types of asymmetries between first/second and third person, Alexiadou (2003:25) comments that "in some languages 3rd person is actually 'non-person'."

There are two problems with Pan's observation, however. First, if it were correct, we would expect subject *pro*-drop in Chinese to behave like subject *pro*-drop in Finnish in being licensed only by first and second person, third person being a "nonperson." But the data on *pro*-drop in the literature do not show this distinction, allowing *pro*-drop with all persons. Second, a number of native Chinese speakers consulted about the data strongly favored the local antecedent, suggesting that for these speakers, there is a blocking effect even with a third-person nominal.

On the other hand, the possibility that first and second person function as the genuine agreement in Chinese is interesting given that there is no morphological manifestation of this agreement and that the language learner has to figure it out essentially from the default setting of Universal Grammar. Is this default setting not just that person agreement is the primary agreement, but in fact that within this category, first- and second-person agreement, which might reflect the discourse nature of the origin of agreement, hold primacy? I leave this issue open.

12. Another well-known case of LDA is found in Icelandic. I will note the core data here, and one recent proposal. The following data (from Boeckx 2008) provide the basic facts (see, e.g., Sigurðsson 1991, 1996, Taraldsen 1995, 1996).

(i) Henni voru gefnar bækurnar.
   she.DAT were.PL given.PL books.NOM.PL
   'She was given the books.'

As shown, when the subject has the quirky dative case, the object receives nominative Case and the verb agrees with this object in number. This is LDA. If the subject is nominative, the agreement goes with the subject and includes person as well as number.

(ii) Við kusum *hún/hana.
   we.NOM elected.1PL she.NOM/her.ACC
   'We elected her.'

With the quirky-case example, the agreement between the verb and the object is limited to number; inserting person agreement leads to ungrammaticality.

(iii) *Henni leiddumst við.
   her.DAT bored.1PL us.NOM
   'She was bored with us.'

Focusing on the fact that person agreement is impossible in LDA, Boeckx (2008) observes that agreements that occur inside vP tend not to have person agreement, and he suggests that (i) is in fact not a case of LDA but a case of agreement inside vP. This is possible, although there are well-known cases of person agreement that involve elements inside vP (see Baker 2008 for example). I leave the issue of Icelandic open.

13. Regarding the idea that complementizer agreement occurs at PF by string adjacency, Liliane Haegeman has pointed to me that, although it is true that the subject must typically be adjacent to the complementizer in West Flemish, there are two exceptions. One is that the object clitic may occur on the complementizer.

(i) ...dan   t   Valère en Marie a   weten.
      that.PL it.CL Valère and Marie already know
   '...that Valère and Marie already know.'

The other is *tet*, a pronounlike particle that may intervene between the complementizer and the subject in finite clauses.

(ii) ...dan   tet Valère en Marie da   weten.
       that.PL TET Valère and Marie that know
   '...that Valère and Marie know.'

We need not consider the object clitic as a counterexample to the need for string adjacency, given that it cliticizes to C. On the other hand, *tet* is apparently not a clitic; I will leave its intervention between subject and complementizer as an issue to be addressed in the future. See Guéron and Haegeman 2007, Haegeman 2008, and Haegeman and Van de Velde 2008 for discussion about *tet*.

Chapter 3

1. The relevance of focus for scrambling has been suggested in Abe 2003, Bailyn 2003, Ishihara 2000, Jung 2002, Miyagawa 1997, 2006, 2007, Otsuka 2005, and Yang 2004, among other works. Kitahara (1994) first suggested that scrambling involves what today we would call minimal Attract, which assumes some sort of feature.

2. Following Aoyagi (1998, 2006; see Sells 1995 for the original idea), I assume that the particle *mo* attaches to the DP (or some other XP) as something like a clitic, thereby not changing the original category's identity as DP, PP, and so on.

3. To be precise, Hasegawa (2005) adopts the idea in Miyagawa 2005b that the focus feature begins at C but is inherited by T, where it attracts the *mo* phrase.

4. In chapter 4, I will introduce an analysis of A- and Ā-movement that allows A-movements to optionally leave a full copy. On this account, there is a further reason why the A-moved focused element does not reconstruct: the A-moved element carries the information-structural element of focus, so that this A-moved chain involving focus is deprived of the option of leaving a trace (see É. Kiss 1998 for relevant discussion about narrow focus and lack of reconstruction).

5. This analysis also responds to a point made about an earlier version of Miyagawa and Arikawa 2007 by Hoji and Ishii (2004)—namely, that the higher position is not an Ā-position. Hoji and Ishii are correct, but with the revision I have introduced in this monograph, their point no longer needs to be considered as a criticism of the overall approach in Miyagawa and Arikawa 2007.

6. Kuroda (1988) was the first to propose that, for example, the object in Japanese can move to Spec,TP. In his approach, this movement is purely optional, but in the approach taken in Miyagawa 2001, it is one way of obligatorily fulfilling the EPP requirement, which can be achieved by moving the object or subject or some other category into Spec,TP. See Kitahara 2002 for an analysis of scrambling that also utilizes the EPP feature on T.

7. Yoshimura (1994) presents some SOV sentences in which the subject has the other nominative marking, *no*. Kato (2007) notes that this *no* independently appears in honorific environments, and Yoshimura's examples involve such honorification. Otherwise, the subject in SOV must have *ga*.

8. There is acquisition evidence in Japanese for the "theme" view of scrambling. In an early study on acquisition of scrambling in Japanese, Hayashibe (1975) noted that there appears to be a period, sometimes up to five years of age, where children tend to interpret scrambled sentences like (ib) as if they were nonscrambled sentences like (ia).

(i) a. *SOV*
   Kamesan-ga ahirusan-o osimasita.
   turtle-NOM   duck-ACC   pushed
   'A turtle pushed a duck.'
   b. *OSV*
   Ahirusan-o kamesan-ga osimasita.
   duck-ACC   turtle-NOM   pushed

Hayashibe concludes from this that scrambling is acquired late in language development. However, Otsu (1994) challenges this assumption by questioning Hayashibe's experimental design. Otsu shows that children even before the age of three have no problem with scrambling when they are presented with a discourse context that makes the scrambled sentence sound natural. The following is an example used in Otsu's experiment:

(ii) Kooen-ni ahirusan-ga imasita. Sono ahirusan-o kamesan-ga osimasita.
   park-in   duck-NOM   was   the   duck-ACC   turtle-NOM   pushed
   'There was a duck in the park. A turtle pushed the duck.'

As is clear, the first sentence registers 'duck' in the discourse, which makes it possible for it to be the theme (also discourse topic) in the second sentence, and in turn making the scrambling of 'duck' natural. This suggests that scrambling must be motivated. It also shows that scrambling emerges early in language development, something not at all surprising if it is akin to grammatical agreement, which is apparently acquired quite early (e.g., Hoekstra and Hyams 1998, Wexler 1998). In chapter 4, I discuss the function of the feature "topic" in detail.

Chapter 4

1. A reviewer points out that, although the noted data are consistent with the idea that Case is active in Kinande, other issues might conspire to give rise to the data without requiring us to adopt the Case analysis. For example, it is well known

that the object reversal construction has a complex set of information-structural properties: although the agreed-with object is a topic, the subject that remains postverbal must be contrastive. These facts are still poorly understood; possibly, with a deeper understanding of them, we will be able to explain the lack of object reversal (and locative reversal) in certain constructions without resorting to Case.

2. A reviewer notes that for (33), it is possible to have an agreement marker for subject along with the agreement marker for *wh*-phrase if the subject is an empty *pro*. According to the reviewer, this is noted in work by Kasangati Kinyalolo. Such a "double-agreement" structure would be possible under the current analysis precisely in the environment of *pro*-drop in the following way. First, two φ-probes are merged at C. One φ-probe lowers to α and is valued by the *wh*-phrase on its way to C, as already noted. The other φ-probe lowers to T. This φ-probe is valued by the agreement head in Spec,vP, just as we saw for *pro*-drop in Greek and other languages in chapter 2. This head does not cause a Minimality violation for the movement of the *wh*-phrase precisely because it is a head, and not an XP. This recalls Anagnostopoulou's (2003) analysis of the Greek double-object construction, in which the theme can be passivized over the dative only if the dative is a clitic, thus a head.

3. I am grateful to Anders Holmberg for assistance with Finnish. All mistakes are my own responsibility.

4. See Sportiche 1999, 2006 for ideas that are similar in the overall rationale although not in the implementation.

5. Thanks to Kyle Johnson for the suggestion that led to this example.

6. Thanks to David Pesetsky for modeling this English example on the original Japanese sentence (64). Kyle Johnson presented examples in his fall 2008 lectures at MIT that had similar properties.

7. I thank Noam Chomsky for suggesting (75) and Kyle Johnson for suggesting an example similar to (76).

8. There are speakers who can get the partial negation interpretation for (77a). However, as noted in Miyagawa and Arikawa 2007, this interpretation appears to be possible with a nondefault prosody; with the default prosody, it is difficult, if not impossible. See Ishihara 2007 for relevant discussion about prosody in this construction.

Chapter 5

1. For a promising approach to *wh*-movement languages and *wh*-in-situ languages based on prosodic considerations, see Richards, to appear.

2. A reviewer raises the question of what triggers the operator movement in relative clauses. The reviewer then suggests as one possibility that it may be topic, as opposed to focus in *wh*-questions, that triggers this movement. This is plausible. Kuno (1973) notes a number of parallels in Japanese between topicalization and relativization. Pesetsky and Torrego (2006) suggest that certain forms of relativization involve topicalization, although the cases they discuss are those that do

not involve *wh*-movement (*the book I read*). Finally, there is a possible correlation between topicalization and WCO. As Chomsky (1982) notes, *wh*-movement within a relative clause does not trigger a WCO violation (*the boy who his mother loves*). Independently, Lasnik and Stowell (1991) point out that topicalization does not trigger a WCO violation. I will not pursue relativization and topicalization further here. These observations provide the interesting possibility that *wh*-movement is triggered by the −focus feature, which remains −focus (topic) in relative clauses but is valued as +focus (focus) in *wh*-questions.

3. Some native speakers might find this example only marginally awkward. For these speakers, a clearer judgment obtains if we add 'almost'.

(i) *Hotondo daremo-ga   nani-o   katta   no?
    almost   everyone-NOM what-ACC bought Q
    'What did almost everyone buy?'

4. Rizzi's (1992) and Pesetsky's (2000) idea that a phonologically null element moves for *wh*-in-situ recalls Watanabe's (1992) analysis of *wh*-in-situ.

5. In a similar vein, Tomioka (2007) notes that the set of intervenors in Japanese is not a natural class. He develops a pragmatic approach to intervention in which the intervenors are what he calls "antitopic" items that, in the intervention environment, are inappropriately forced into a topic position.

6. The etymology of *ka* in the NPI *sika* is not known (Konoshima 1983). I will simply assume that this *ka* is the same *ka* as those in the existential expressions.

7. See Lee 2004 for an extensive discussion of similar constructions in Korean.

8. What we just observed may also explain what has been termed scope rigidity in Japanese—the notion that quantifier scope is limited to surface scope and inverse scope is impossible (Hoji 1985, Kuroda 1971). The quantifiers most commonly used from early on to show this are typically existential and universal quantifiers marked by *ka* and *mo*, respectively. Some linguists have informally observed that inverse scope is easier to obtain with, for example, numerals.

9. As a reviewer notes, if *minna* 'all' is not lexically marked for focus, it should be able to stay inside the scope of negation, a fact confirmed in the following example:

(i) Minna-ga piza-o   tabe-nakat-ta.
    all-NOM   pizza-ACC eat-NEG-PAST
    'All didn't eat pizza.'
    not > all, all > not

10. As a reviewer notes, the other possibility is that the universal quantifier 'everyone/all each' raises to a position high in the structure, higher than the question C, so that intervention never takes place. This is the notion of "quantifying in" (see Beck 1996). This is consistent with the idea that *minna* is not focused; because it doesn't enter into agreement with a probe, it is free to move above the CP by QR. I simply note this alternative; I will not pursue it here.

11. I should note that the original Relativized Minimality approach to intervention is found in Hagstrom 1998:63.

12. In the German intervention case, where no question-particle movement takes place, we could imagine a couple of scenarios. One is the Rizzi-type analysis, in which a piece of the *wh*-phrase that contains the focus feature tries to move to C but is blocked by the intervening focus phrase *niemand* 'nobody'. Alternatively, under the expletive account given earlier, the "expletive" *wh*-phrase *was* merges right above the *wh*-phrase. *Was* takes on the focus feature of the *wh*-phrase, thereby acting as the goal of the focus feature at C. It then tries to move to C to attain PGU, but its movement is blocked by the intervening focus phrase *niemand*.

References

Abe, Jun. 2003. Economy of scrambling. Unpublished manuscript, Tohoku Gaikuin University.

Akmajian, Adrian, and Frank Heny. 1975. *An introduction to the principles of transformational syntax*. Cambridge, Mass.: MIT Press.

Alexiadou, Artemis. 2003. On nominative case features and split agreement. In Ellen Brandner and Heike Zinsmeister, eds., *New perspectives on Case theory*, 23–52. Stanford, Calif.: CSLI Publications.

Alexiadou, Artemis, and Elena Anagnostopoulou. 1998. Parametrizing word order, V-movement, and EPP-checking. *Natural Language & Linguistic Theory* 16:491–539.

Anagnostopoulou, Elena. 2003. *The syntax of ditransitives: Evidence from clitics*. Berlin: Mouton de Gruyter.

Anderson, Stephen. 1992. *A-morphous morphology*. Cambridge: Cambridge University Press.

Aoyagi, Hiroshi. 1998. Particles as adjunct clitics. In Pius Tamanji and Kiyomi Kusumoto, eds., *NELS 28*, 17–31. Amherst: University of Massachusetts, Graduate Linguistic Student Association.

Aoyagi, Hiroshi. 2006. *Nihongo no joshi to kinoohanchu* [Particles and functional categories in Japanese]. Tokyo: Hituzi Syobo.

Archangeli, Diana, and Douglas Pulleyblank. 1987. Maximal and minimal rules: The effects of tier scansion. In Joyce McDonough and Bernadette Plunkett, eds., *NELS 17*, 16–35. Amherst: University of Massachusetts, Graduate Linguistic Student Association.

Bahloul, Maher, and Wayne Harbert. 1993. Agreement asymmetries in Arabic. In Jonathan Mead, ed., *WCCFL 11*, 15–31. Stanford, Calif.: CSLI Publications.

Bailyn, John F. 2003. Does Russian scrambling exist? In Simin Karimi, ed., *Word order and scrambling*, 156–176. Oxford: Blackwell.

Baker, C. L. 1970. Notes on the description of English questions: The role of an abstract question morpheme. *Foundations of Language* 6:197–219.

Baker, Mark. 1996. *The polysynthesis parameter*. Oxford: Oxford University Press.

Baker, Mark. 2003. Agreement, dislocation, and partial configurationality. In Andrew Carnie, Heidi Harley, and MaryAnn Willie, eds., *Formal approaches to function in grammar*, 107–132. Amsterdam: John Benjamins.

Baker, Mark. 2008. *The syntax of agreement and concord*. Cambridge: Cambridge University Press.

Battistella, Edwin. 1989. Chinese reflexivization: A movement to INFL approach. *Linguistics* 27:987–1012.

Beck, Sigrid. 1995. Negative islands and reconstruction. In Uli Lutz and Jürgen Pafel, eds., *Extraction and extraposition in German*, 121–143. Amsterdam: John Benjamins.

Beck, Sigrid. 1996. Quantified structures as barriers for LF movement. *Natural Language Semantics* 4:1–56.

Beck, Sigrid. 2006. Intervention effects follow from focus interpretation. *Natural Language Semantics* 14:1–56.

Beck, Sigrid, and Shin-Sook Kim. 1997. On *wh-* and operator scope in Korean. *Journal of East Asian Linguistics* 6:339–384.

Beck, Sigrid, and Hotze Rullmann. 1998. Presupposition projection and the interpretation of *which* questions. In Devon Strolovitch and Aaron Lawson, eds., *SALT 8*, 215–232. Ithaca, N.Y.: Cornell University, CLC Publications.

Belletti, Adriana. 1990. *Generalized verb movement*. Turin: Rosenberg and Sellier.

Benmamoun, Elabbas. 1992. Functional and inflectional morphology: Problems of projection, representation, and derivation. Doctoral dissertation, University of Southern California, Los Angeles.

Bhatt, Rajesh. 2005. Long distance agreement in Hindi-Urdu. *Natural Language & Linguistic Theory* 23:757–807.

Bhatt, Rajesh, and Roumyana Pancheva. 2004. Late merger of degree clauses. *Linguistic Inquiry* 35:1–45.

Bhatt, Rajesh, and Roumyana Pancheva. 2007. Degree quantifiers, positions of merger effects with their restrictors, and conservativity. In Chris Barker and Pauline Jacobson, eds., *Direct compositionality*, 306–335. Oxford: Oxford University Press.

Blake, Barry. 1990. *Relational Grammar*. London: Croom Helm.

Blight, Ralph C. 1999. Verb positions and the auxiliary *be*. Unpublished manuscript, University of Texas, Austin.

Bobaljik, Jonathan David. 2006. Where's phi? Agreement as a post-syntactic operation [working paper version]. In Marjo van Koppen, Pepijn Hendriks, Frank Landsbergen, Mika Poss, and Jenneke van der Wal, eds., *Leiden working papers in linguistics* 3(2), 1–23. Leiden: Leiden University Centre for Linguistics.

Bobaljik, Jonathan David, and Susi Wurmbrand. 2005. The domain of agreement. *Natural Language & Linguistic Theory* 23:809–865.

Boeckx, Cedric. 2000. Quirky agreement. *Studia Linguistica* 54:354–380.

Boeckx, Cedric. 2003. *Islands and chains: Resumption as stranding*. Amsterdam: John Benjamins.

Boeckx, Cedric. 2007. Case and agreement: The syntax of A-dependencies. Unpublished manuscript, Harvard University.

Boeckx, Cedric. 2008. *Aspects of the syntax of agreement*. London: Routledge.

Bošković, Željko. 1997. *The syntax of nonfinite complementation*. Cambridge, Mass.: MIT Press.

Bošković, Željko. 2002. A-movement and the EPP. *Syntax* 5:167–218.

Bowers, John. 1993. The syntax of predication. *Linguistic Inquiry* 24:591–656.

Brandi, Luciana, and Patricia Cordin. 1989. Two Italian dialects and the null subject parameter. In Osvaldo Jaeggli and Kenneth J. Safir, eds., *The null subject parameter*, 111–142. Dordrecht: Kluwer.

Bresnan, Joan. 2001. *Lexical-Functional Syntax*. Oxford: Blackwell.

Brody, Michael. 1990. Remarks on the order of elements in the Hungarian focus field. In István Kenesei, ed., *Approaches to Hungarian 3*, 95–121. Szeged: JATE.

Burzio, Luigi. 1986. *Italian syntax: A Government-Binding approach*. Dordrecht: Reidel.

Cable, Seth. 2007. The Grammar of Q: Q-Particles and the Nature of *Wh*-Fronting, as Revealed by the *Wh*-Questions of Tlingit. Doctoral dissertation, MIT.

Caponigro, Ivano, and Carson T. Schütze. 2003. Parameterizing passive participle movement. *Linguistic Inquiry* 34:293–308.

Carstens, Vicki. 2003. Rethinking complementizer agreement: Agree with a case-checked goal. *Linguistic Inquiry* 34:393–412.

Carstens, Vicki. 2005. Agree and EPP in Bantu. *Natural Language & Linguistic Theory* 23:219–279.

Chang, Lisa. 1997. *Wh*-in-situ phenomena in French. Master's thesis, University of British Columbia.

Cheng, Lisa L.-S. 1991. On the typology of *wh*-questions. Doctoral dissertation, MIT.

Chierchia, Gennaro. 1998. Reference to kinds across languages. *Natural Language Semantics* 6:339–405.

Choe, Hyon Sook. 2006. The syntax of existential *there* and the structure of nominal expressions. Unpublished manuscript, MIT/Yeungnam University.

Chomsky, Noam. 1955/1975. *Logical structure of linguistic theory*. New York: Plenum.

Chomsky, Noam. 1965. *Aspects of the theory of syntax*. Cambridge, Mass.: MIT Press.

Chomsky, Noam. 1981. *Lectures on government and binding*. Dordrecht: Foris.

Chomsky, Noam. 1986. *Reflections on language*. New York: Pantheon.

Chomsky, Noam. 1993. A minimalist program for linguistic theory. In Kenneth Hale and Samuel Jay Keyser, eds., *The view from Building 20*, 1–52. Cambridge, Mass.: MIT Press.

Chomsky, Noam. 1995. *The Minimalist Program*. Cambridge, Mass.: MIT Press.

Chomsky, Noam. 2000. Minimalist inquiries. In Roger Martin, David Michaels, and Juan Uriagereka, eds., *Step by step: Essays on minimalism in honor of Howard Lasnik*, 89–155. Cambridge, Mass.: MIT Press.

Chomsky, Noam. 2001. Derivation by phase. In Michael Kenstowicz, ed., *Ken Hale: A life in language*, 1–52. Cambridge, Mass.: MIT Press.

Chomsky, Noam. 2005. Three factors in language design. *Linguistic Inquiry* 36:1–22.

Chomsky, Noam. 2007. Approaching UG from below. In Uli Sauerland and Hans-Martin Gärtner, eds., *Interfaces + recursion = language?: Chomsky's minimalism and the view from syntax-semantics*, 1–29. Berlin: Mouton de Gruyter.

Chomsky, Noam. 2008. On phases. In Robert Freidin, Carlos Otero, and Maria Luisa Zubizarreta, eds., *Foundational issues in linguistic theory*, 133–166. Cambridge, Mass.: MIT Press.

Chung, Sandra. 1998. *The design of agreement: Evidence from Chamorro*. Chicago: University of Chicago Press.

Cinque, Guglielmo. 1999. *Adverbs and functional heads: A cross-linguistic perspective*. Oxford: Oxford University Press.

Cole, Peter, Gabriella Hermon, and Li-May Sung. 1990. Principles and parameters of long-distance reflexives. *Linguistic Inquiry* 21:1–22.

Corbett, Greville G. 2006. *Agreement*. Cambridge: Cambridge University Press.

Culicover, Peter, and Michael Rochemont. 1983. Stress and focus in English. *Language* 59:123–165.

Diesing, Molly. 1992. *Indefinites*. Cambridge, Mass.: MIT Press.

Elouazizi, Noureddine. 2005. Anti-agreement effects as (anti)-connectivity. In John Alderete, Chung-hye Han, and Alexei Kochetov, eds., *WCCFL 24*, 120–128. Somerville, Mass.: Cascadilla Proceedings Project.

Emonds, Joseph. 1976. *A transformational approach to English syntax*. New York: Academic Press.

Engdahl, Elisabet. 1985. Parasitic gaps, resumptive pronouns, and subject extractions. *Linguistics* 23:3–44.

Epstein, Samuel David, and T. Daniel Seely. 1999. SPEC-ifying the GF 'subject': Eliminating A-chains and the EPP within a derivational model. Unpublished manuscript, University of Michigan and Eastern Michigan University.

Fassi Fehri, Abdelkader. 1993. *Issues in the structure of Arabic clauses and word order*. Dordrecht: Kluwer.

Fox, Danny. 1999. Reconstruction, binding theory, and the interpretation of chains. *Linguistic Inquiry* 30:157–196.

Fox, Danny. 2000. *Economy and semantic interpretation*. Cambridge, Mass.: MIT Press.

Fox, Danny. 2002. Antecedent-contained deletion and the copy theory of movement. *Linguistic Inquiry* 33:63–96.

Freidin, Robert. 1986. Fundamental issues in the theory of binding. In Barbara Lust, ed., *Studies in the acquisition of anaphora*, 151–188. Dordrecht: Reidel.

Fukui, Naoki. 1986. A theory of category projection and its applications. Doctoral dissertation, MIT.

Gazdar, Gerald, Ewan Klein, Geoffrey Pullum, and Ivan Sag. 1985. *Generalized Phrase Structure Grammar.* Cambridge, Mass.: Harvard University Press.

George, Leland, and Jaklin Kornfilt. 1981. Finiteness and boundedness in Turkish. In Frank Heny, ed., *Binding and filtering*, 105–127. London: Croom Helm, and Cambridge, Mass.: MIT Press.

Givón, Talmy. 1976. Topic, pronoun and grammatical agreement. In Charles Li, ed., *Subject and topic*, 149–188. New York: Academic Press.

Grewendorf, Günther. 2005. The discourse configurationality of scrambling. In Joachim Sabel and Mamoru Saito, eds., *The free word order phenomenon: Its syntactic sources and diversity*, 75–136. Berlin: Mouton de Gruyter.

Guéron, Jacqueline, and Liliane Haegeman. 2007. Subject positions, point of view, and the neuter pronoun *tet* in West Flemish. Unpublished manuscript, Paris III and STL Lille III.

Haegeman, Liliane. 1992. Some speculations on argument shift, clitics and crossing in West Flemish. Unpublished manuscript, University of Geneva.

Haegeman, Liliane. 2008. Pleonastic *tet* in West Flemish and the cartography of subject positions. In Sjef Barbiers, Margreet van der Ham, Olaf Koeneman, and Marika Lekakou, eds., *Microvariations in syntactic doubling*, 277–290. Amsterdam: Elsevier.

Haegeman, Liliane, and Danièle Van de Velde. 2008. Pleonastic *tet* in the Lapscheure dialect. *Catalan Journal of Lingsuistics* 7:157–199.

Hagstrom, Paul. 1998. Decomposing questions. Doctoral dissertation, MIT.

Haig, John H. 1980. Some observations on quantifier floating in Japanese. *Linguistics* 18:1065–1083.

Halle, Morris, and Alec Marantz. 1993. Distributed Morphology and the pieces of inflection. In Kenneth Hale and Samuel Jay Keyser, eds., *The view from Building 20*, 111–176. Cambridge, Mass.: MIT Press.

Hamblin, Charles Leonard. 1973. Questions in Montague English. *Foundations of Language* 10:41–53.

Hasegawa, Nobuko. 1991. Affirmative polarity items and negation in Japanese. In Carol Georgopoulos and Roberta Ishihara, eds., *Interdisciplinary approaches to language: Essays in honor of S.-Y. Kuroda*, 271–285. Dordrecht: Kluwer.

Hasegawa, Nobuko. 1994. Economy of derivation and Ā-movement in Japanese. In Masaru Nakamura, ed., *Current topics in English and Japanese*, 1–25. Tokyo: Hituzi Syobo.

Hasegawa, Nobuko. 2005. The EPP materialized first, Agree later: *Wh*-questions, subjects and *mo* 'also'-phrases. *Scientific Approaches to Language* 4:33–88.

Hayashibe, Hideo. 1975. Word order and particles: A developmental study in Japanese. *Descriptive and Applied Linguistics* 8:1–18.

Heim, Irene. 1982. The semantics of definite and indefinite noun phrases. Doctoral dissertation, University of Massachusetts, Amherst.

Hoekstra, Jarich, and László Marácz. 1989. On the position of inflection in West Germanic. *Working Papers in Scandinavian Syntax* 44:75–88.

Hoekstra, Teun, and Nina Hyams. 1998. Aspects of root infinitives. *Lingua* 106:81–112.

Hoji, Hajime. 1985. Logical Form constraints and configurational structures in Japanese. Doctoral dissertation, University of Washington, Seattle.

Hoji, Hajime, and Yasuo Ishii. 2004. What gets mapped to the tripartite structure of quantification in Japanese. In Vineeta Chand, Ann Kelleher, Angelo J. Rodríguex, and Benjamin Schmeiser, eds., *WCCFL 23*, 346–359. Somerville, Mass.: Cascadilla Press.

Holmberg, Anders. 2005. Is there a little pro? Evidence from Finnish. *Linguistic Inquiry* 36:533–564.

Holmberg, Anders, and Urpo Nikanne. 2002. Expletives, subjects, and topics in Finnish. In Peter Svenonius, ed., *Subjects, expletives, and the EPP*, 71–106. Oxford: Oxford University Press.

Horvath, Julia. 1981. Aspects of Hungarian syntax and the theory of grammar. Doctoral dissertation, UCLA.

Horvath, Julia. 1986. *FOCUS in the theory of grammar and the syntax of Hungarian*. Dordrecht: Foris.

Horvath, Julia. 1995. Structural focus, structural Case, and the notion of feature-assignment. In Katalin É. Kiss, ed., *Discourse configurational languages*, 28–64. Oxford: Oxford University Press.

Huang, C.-T. James. 1982. Logical relations in Chinese and the theory of grammar. Doctoral dissertation, MIT.

Huang, C.-T. James. 1984. On the distribution and reference of empty pronouns. *Linguistic Inquiry* 15:531–574.

Huang, C.-T. James, and C.-C. Jane Tang. 1991. The local nature of the long-distance reflexive in Chinese. In Jan Koster and Eric Reuland, eds., *Long-distance anaphora*, 263–282. Cambridge: Cambridge University Press.

Huang, Yun-Hua. 1984. Reflexives in Chinese. *Studies in English Literature and Linguistics* 10:163–188.

Iatridou, Sabine. 1993. On nominative case assignment and a few related things. In Colin Phillips, ed., *Papers on Case and agreement II*, 175–196. MIT Working Papers in Linguistics 19. Cambridge, Mass.: MIT, MIT Working Papers in Linguistics.

Inoue, Kazuko. 2006. Nihongo-no jookenbun-to shubun-no modaritii [Conditional construction and modality in the matrix clause in Japanese]. *Scientific Approaches to Language* 5:9–28.

Ishihara, Shinichiro. 2000. Stress, focus, and scrambling in Japanese. In Elena Guerzoni and Ora Matushansky, eds., *A few from Building E39: Papers in syntax, semantics, and their interface*, 142–175. MIT Working Papers in Linguistics 39. Cambridge, Mass.: MIT, MIT Working Papers in Linguistics.

Ishihara, Shinichiro. 2007. Major phrase, focus intonation, and multiple spell-out. *The Linguistic Review* 24:137–167.

Isobe, Yoshihiro. 1990. Chuuko-wabun-no yoosetsumei gimonhyoogen [Question expressions in Middle Japanese]. *Nihon-Bungaku Kenkyuu* 26:165–176.

Jacobsen, Bent, and Per Anker Jensen. 1982. Some remarks on Danish weakly stressed *der*. Unpublished manuscript, Aarhus Business School.

Jaeggli, Osvaldo. 1982. *Topics in Romance syntax*. Dordrecht: Foris.

Jespersen, Otto. 1924. *The philosophy of grammar*. London: George Allen and Unwin.

Johnson, Kyle. 1991. Object positions. *Natural Language & Linguistic Theory* 9:577–636.

Jung, Yeun-Jin. 2002. Scrambling, edge effects, and A/Ā-distinction. *The Linguistics Association of Korea Journal* 10(4):41–64.

Karttunen, Lauri. 1977. Syntax and semantics of questions. *Linguistics and Philosophy* 1:3–44.

Kato, Sachiko. 2007. Scrambling and the EPP in Japanese: From the viewpoint of the Kumamoto dialect in Japanese. In *Formal Approaches to Japanese Linguistics: Proceedings of FAJL 4*, 113–124. MIT Working Papers in Linguistics 55. Cambridge, Mass.: MIT, MIT Working Papers in Linguistics.

Kato, Yasuhiko. 1988. Negation and the discourse-dependent property of relative scope in Japanese. *Sophia Linguistica* 23:31–37. Tokyo: Sophia University.

Kayne, Richard. 1984. *Connectedness and binary branching*. Dordrecht: Foris.

Kayne, Richard. 1994. *The antisymmetry of syntax*. Cambridge, Mass.: MIT Press.

Kayne, Richard. 2006. Expletives, datives, and the tension between morphology and syntax. Unpublished manuscript, New York University.

Keenan, Edward. 1974. The functional principle: Generalizing the notion 'subject of'. In Michael W. La Galy, Robert A. Fox, and Anthony Bruck, eds., *Papers from the 10th Regional Meeting of the Chicago Linguistic Society*, 298–309. Chicago: University of Chicago, Chicago Linguistic Society.

Kenstowicz, Michael. 1989. The null subject parameter in modern Arabic dialects. In Osvaldo Jaeggli and Kenneth J. Safir, eds., *The null subject parameter*, 263–275. Dordrecht: Kluwer.

Kim, Shin-Sook. 2002. Intervention effects are focus effects. In Noriko Akatsuka and Susan Strauss, eds., *Japanese/Korean linguistics 10*, 615–628. Stanford, Calif.: CSLI Publications.

Kim, Shin-Sook. 2006. Questions, focus, and intervention effects. In Susumu Kuno et al., eds., *Harvard studies in Korean linguistics 11*, 520–533. Cambridge, Mass.: Harvard University, Department of Linguistics.

Kinyalolo, Kasangati K. W. 1991. Syntactic dependencies and the Spec-head agreement hypothesis in Kilega. Doctoral dissertation, UCLA.

Kishimoto, Hideki. 2001. Binding of indeterminate pronouns and clause structure in Japanese. *Linguistic Inquiry* 32:597–633.

Kishimoto, Hideki. 2005. *Wh*-in-situ and movement in Sinhala questions. *Natural Language & Linguistic Theory* 23:1–51.

Kishimoto, Hideki. 2006. Japanese as a topic-movement language. *Scientific Approaches to Language* 5:85–105.

É. Kiss, Katalin. 1995. Introduction. In Katalin É. Kiss, ed., *Discourse configurational languages*, 3–27. Oxford: Oxford University Press.

É. Kiss, Katalin. 1997. Discourse-configurationality in the languages of Europe. In Anna Siewierska, ed., *Constituent order in the languages of Europe*, 681–727. Berlin: Mouton de Gruyter.

É. Kiss, Katalin. 1998. Identificational focus versus informational focus. *Language* 74:245–273.

É. Kiss, Katalin. 2003. Argument scrambling, operator movement, and topic movement in Hungarian. In Simin Karimi, ed., *Word order and scrambling*, 22–43. Oxford: Blackwell.

Kitagawa, Yoshihisa. 1986. Subject in Japanese and English. Doctoral dissertation, University of Massachusetts, Amherst.

Kitahara, Hisatsugu. 1994. Restricting ambiguous rule-application: A unified analysis of movement. In Masatoshi Koizumi and Hiroyuki Ura, eds., *Formal Approaches to Japanese Linguistics: Proceedings of FAJL 1*, 179–209. MIT Working Papers in Linguistics 24. Cambridge, Mass.: MIT, MIT Working Papers in Linguistics.

Kitahara, Hisatsugu. 2002. Scrambling, Case, and interpretability. In Samuel David Epstein and T. Daniel Seely, eds., *Derivation and explanation in the Minimalist Program*, 167–183. Oxford: Blackwell.

Klima, Edward. 1964. Negation in English. In Jerry A. Fodor and Jerrold Katz, eds., *The structure of language*, 246–323. Englewood Cliffs, N.J.: Prentice-Hall.

Ko, Heejeong. 2007. Asymmetries in scrambling and cyclic linearization. *Linguistic Inquiry* 38:49–83.

Koizumi, Masatoshi. 1995. Phrase structure in minimalist syntax. Doctoral dissertation, MIT.

Koizumi, Masatoshi. 2008. Nominative object. In Shigeru Miyagawa and Mamoru Saito, eds., *The Oxford handbook of Japanese linguistics*, 141–164. Oxford: Oxford University Press.

Kokinshuu. 1975. Tokyo: Shintensha.

Konoshima, M. 1983. *Jodooshi, joshi gaisetsu* [Auxiliary verbs and case marking: An outline]. Tokyo: Ofusha.

Koopman, Hilda. 2000. *The syntax of specifiers and heads: Collected essays of Hilda J. Koopman*. New York: Routledge.

Koopman, Hilda. 2003. Inside the "noun" in Maasai. In Anoop Mahajan, ed., *Syntax at sunset 3: Head movement and syntactic theory*, 77–116. Los Angeles: UCLA, Department of Linguistics.

Koopman, Hilda. 2005. Agreement: In defense of "Spec head." In Cedric Boeckx, ed., *Agreement systems*, 159–199. Amsterdam: John Benjamins.

Koopman, Hilda, and Dominique Sportiche. 1991. The position of subjects. *Lingua* 85:211–258.

Koppen, Marjo van. 2006. Complementizer agreement and the relation between C^0 and T^0. Unpublished manuscript, Utrecht University.

Kornfilt, Jaklin. 2000. Some syntactic and morphological properties of relative clauses in Turkish. In Artemis Alexiadou, Chris Wilder, and Paul Law, eds., *The syntax of relative clauses*, 121–159. Amsterdam: John Benjamins.

Kornfilt, Jaklin. 2004. Unmasking covert complementizer agreement. Paper presented at the annual meeting of the Linguistic Society of America, Boston, 10 January.

Kratzer, Angelika, and Junko Shimoyama. 2002. Indeterminate pronouns: The view from Japanese. In Yukio Otsu, ed., *Proceedings of the 3rd Tokyo Conference on Psycholinguistics*, 1–25. Tokyo: Keio University.

Kuno, Susumu. 1973. *The structure of the Japanese language*. Cambridge, Mass.: MIT Press.

Kuroda, S.-Y. 1965. Generative grammatical studies in the Japanese language. Doctoral dissertation, MIT.

Kuroda, S.-Y. 1971. Remarks on the notion of subject with reference to words like *also*, *even*, or *only*, illustrating certain manners in which formal systems are employed as auxiliary devices in linguistic descriptions: Part 2. *Annual Bulletin 4*, Logopedics and Phoniatrics Research Institute, University of Tokyo, 127–152. [Reprinted in *Papers in Japanese Linguistics* 11:157–202.]

Kuroda, S.-Y. 1972–1973. The categorical and the thetic judgment. *Foundations of Language* 9:153–185.

Kuroda, S.-Y. 1980. Bun kouzou no hikaku [The comparison of sentence structures]. In Tetsuya Kunihiro, ed., *Niti-eigo hikaku kouza 2: Bunpou* [Lectures on Japanese-English comparative studies 2: Grammar], 23–61. Tokyo: Taisyukan.

Kuroda, S.-Y. 1988. Whether we agree or not: A comparative syntax of English and Japanese. *Lingvisticae Investigationes* 12:1–47.

Lahiri, Utpal. 1998. Focus and negative polarity in Hindi. *Natural Language Semantics* 6:57–123.

Laka, Itziar. 1990. Negation in syntax: On the nature of functional categories and projections. Doctoral dissertation, MIT.

Landau, Idan. 2007. EPP extensions. *Linguistic Inquiry* 38:485–523.

Lasnik, Howard. 1995. Case and expletives revisited: On Greed and other human failings. *Linguistic Inquiry* 26:615–633.

Lasnik, Howard. 1997. A gap in an ellipsis paradigm: Some theoretical implications. *Linguistic Analysis* 27:166–185.

Lasnik, Howard. 1999a. Chains of arguments. In Samuel David Epstein and Norbert Hornstein, eds., *Working minimalism*, 189–215. Cambridge, Mass.: MIT Press.

Lasnik, Howard. 1999b. *Minimalist analysis*. Oxford: Blackwell.

Lasnik, Howard. 2003. *Miminalist investigations in linguistic theory*. New York: Routledge.

Lasnik, Howard, and Tim Stowell. 1991. Weakest Crossover. *Linguistic Inquiry* 22:687–720.

Lebeaux, David. 1988. Language acquisition and the form of the grammar. Doctoral dissertation, University of Massachusetts, Amherst.

Lee, Youngjoo. 2004. The syntax and semantics of focus particles. Doctoral dissertation, MIT.

Levin, Magnus. 2001. *Agreement with collective nouns in English*. Stockholm: Almqvist & Wiksell.

Li, Charles N., and Sandra A. Thompson. 1981. *Mandarin Chinese: A functional reference grammar*. Los Angeles: University of California Press.

Li, Yen-hui Audrey. 1990. *Order and constituency in Mandarin Chinese*. Dordrecht: Kluwer.

Mahajan, Anoop. 1989. Agreement and agreement phrases. In Itziar Laka and Anoop Mahajan, eds., *Functional heads and clause structure*, 217–252. MIT Working Papers in Linguistics 10. Cambridge, Mass.: MIT, MIT Working Papers in Linguistics.

Mahajan, Anoop. 1990. The A/A′ distinction and movement theory. Doctoral dissertation, MIT.

Maki, Hideki, Lizanne Kaiser, and Masao Ochi. 1999. Embedded topicalization in English and Japanese. *Lingua* 114:809–847.

Marantz, Alec. 1984. *On the nature of grammatical relations*. Cambridge, Mass.: MIT Press.

Martin, Roger. 1999. Case, the EPP, and minimalism. In Samuel David Epstein and Norbert Hornstein, eds., *Working minimalism*, 1–25. Cambridge, Mass.: MIT Press.

Marty, A. 1918. *Gesammelte Schriften II*. Band 1. Halle: Max Niemeyer.

Marty, A. 1965. *Psyche und Sprachstruktur*. Bern: Verlag A. Francke.

Matthewson, Lisa. 2002. An underspecified Tense in St'á'imcets. Paper presented at the Western Conference on Linguistics, University of British Columbia, 1–3 November.

May, Robert. 1977. The grammar of quantification. Doctoral dissertation, MIT.

McCloskey, James. 1996. On the scope of verb-movement in Irish. *Natural Language & Linguistic Theory* 14:47–104.

McCloskey, James. 2001. The distribution of subject properties in Irish. In William Davies and Stanley Dubinsky, eds., *Objects and other subjects: Grammatical functions, functional categories, and configurationality*, 157–192. Dordrecht: Kluwer.

McDaniel, Dana. 1989. Partial and multiple *wh*-movement. *Natural Language & Linguistic Theory* 7:565–604.

Milsark, Gary. 1974. Existential sentences in English. Doctoral dissertation, MIT.

Miyagawa, Shigeru. 1993. LF Case-checking and Minimal Link Condition. In Colin Phillips, ed., *Case and agreement II*, 213–254. MIT Working Papers in Lingustics 19. Cambridge, Mass.: MIT, MIT Working Papers in Linguistics.

Miyagawa, Shigeru. 1997. Against optional scrambling. *Linguistic Inquiry* 28:1–26.

Miyagawa, Shigeru. 1998. On *wh*-scope. Unpublished manuscript, MIT.

Miyagawa, Shigeru. 2001. The EPP, scrambling, and *wh*-in-situ. In Michael Kenstowicz, ed., *Ken Hale: A life in language*. Cambridge, Mass.: MIT Press.

Miyagawa, Shigeru. 2003. A-movement scrambling and options without optionality. In Simin Karimi, ed., *Word order and scrambling*, 177–200. Oxford: Blackwell.

Miyagawa, Shigeru. 2005a. EPP and semantically vacuous scrambling. In Joachim Sabel and Mamoru Saito, eds., *The free word order phenomenon*, 181–220. Berlin: Mouton de Gruyter.

Miyagawa, Shigeru. 2005b. On the EPP. In Martha McGinnis and Norvin Richards, eds., *Perspectives on phases*, 201–236. MIT Working Papers in Linguistics 49. Cambridge, Mass.: MIT, MIT Working Papers in Linguistics.

Miyagawa, Shigeru. 2006. On the "undoing" property of scrambling: A response to Bošković. *Linguistic Inquiry* 37:607–624.

Miyagawa, Shigeru. 2007. Unifying agreement and agreementless languages. In Meltem Kelepir and Balkiz Öztürk, eds., *Proceedings of the Workshop on Altaic Formal Linguistics 2*, 47–66. MIT Working Papers in Linguistics 54. Cambridge, Mass.: MIT, MIT Working Papers in Linguistics.

Miyagawa, Shigeru, and Koji Arikawa. 2007. Locality in syntax and floating numeral quantifiers. *Linguistic Inquiry* 38:645–670.

Miyamoto, Yoichi, and Mina Sugimura. 2005. A subject/object asymmetry and its implication for clausal architecture in Japanese. *Nanzan Linguistics* 2:33–46.

Moro, Andrea. 1997. *The raising of predicates*. Cambridge: Cambridge University Press.

Muysken, Pieter. 1982. Parametrizing the notion head. *Journal of Linguistic Research* 2:57–75.

Nishigauchi, Taisuke. 1990. *Quantification in the theory of grammar*. Dordrecht: Kluwer.

Nitta, Yoshio. 1991. *Nihongo-no modaritii-to ninshoo* [Modality and person in Japanese]. Tokyo: Hituzi Syobo.

Nomura, Masashi. 2005. Nominative Case and AGREE(ment). Doctoral dissertation, University of Connecticut, Storrs.

Nomura, Takashi. 1993. Joudaigo no *no* to *ga* nitsuite [*No* and *ga* in Old Japanese]. *Kokugo-Kokubun* 62(2):1–17, 62(3):30–49.

Odden, David. 1994. Adjacency parameters in phonology. *Language* 70:289–330.

Otsu, Yukio. 1994. Early acquisition of scrambling in Japanese. In Teun Hoekstra and Bonnie D. Schwartz, eds., *Language acquisition studies in generative grammar*, 253–264. Amsterdam: John Benjamins.

Otsuka, Yuko. 2005. Scrambling and information focus: VSO-VOS alternation in Tongan. In Joachim Sabel and Mamoru Saito, eds., *The free word order phenomenon: Its syntactic sources and diversity*, 243–280. Berlin: Mouton de Gruyter.

Ouhalla, Jamal. 1993. Subject-extraction, negation, and the anti-agreement effect. *Natural Language & Linguistic Theory* 11:477–518.

Ouhalla, Jamal. 2005. Agreement features, agreement, and anti-agreement. *Natural Language & Linguistic Theory* 23:655–686.

Pak, Miok. 2006. Jussive clauses and agreement of sentence final particles in Korean. In Tim Vance and Kimberly Jones, ed., *Japanese/Korean linguistics 14*, 295–306. Stanford, Calif.: CSLI Publications.

Pan, Haihua. 2000. Why the blocking effect? In Peter Cole, C.-T. James Huang, and Gabriella Hermon, eds., *Long-distance reflexives*, 279–316. San Diego, Calif.: Academic Press.

Perlmutter, David. 1971. *Deep and surface structure constraints in syntax*. New York: Holt, Rinehart and Winston.

Perlmutter, David, and Paul Postal. 1983. The Relational Succession Law. In David Perlmutter, ed., *Studies in Relational Grammar 1*, 30–80. Chicago: University of Chicago Press.

Pesetsky, David. 2000. *Phrasal movement and its kin*. Cambridge, Mass.: MIT Press.

Pesetsky, David, and Esther Torrego. 2001. T-to-C movement: Causes and consequences. In Michael Kenstowicz, ed., *Ken Hale: A life in language*, 355–426. Cambridge, Mass.: MIT Press.

Pesetsky, David, and Esther Torrego. 2006. Probes, goals, and syntactic categories. In Yukio Otsu, ed., *Proceedings of the 7th annual Tokyo Conference on Psycholinguistics*, 25–60. Tokyo: Hituzi Syobo.

Pesetsky, David, and Esther Torrego. 2007. The syntax of valuation and the interpretability of features. In Simin Karimi, Vida Samiian, and Wendy Wilkins, eds., *Phrasal and clausal architecture*, 262–294. Amsterdam: John Benjamins.

Polinsky, Maria, and Eric Potsdam. 2001. Long-distance agreement and topic in Tsez. *Natural Language & Linguistic Theory* 19:583–646.

Pollard, Carl, and Ivan A. Sag. 1994. *Head-Driven Phrase Structure Grammar*. Chicago: University of Chicago Press, and Stanford, Calif.: CSLI Publications.

Pollock, Jean-Yves. 1989. Verb movement, Universal Grammar, and the structure of IP. *Linguistic Inquiry* 20:365–424.

Progovac, Ljiljana. 1993. Negative polarity: Entailment and binding. *Linguistics and Philosophy* 16:149–180.

Ramchand, Gillian. 1997. *Aspect and predication: The semantics of argument structure*. Oxford: Oxford University Press.

Reinhart, Tanya. 1995. *Interface strategies*. Utrecht: OTS Working Papers.

Richards, Norvin. 2001. *Movement in language: Interactions and architectures*. Oxford: Oxford University Press.

Richards, Norvin. To appear. *Uttering trees*. Cambridge, Mass.: MIT Press.

Riemsdijk, Henk van, and Edwin Williams. 1981. NP structure. *The Linguistic Review* 1:171–217.

Rizzi, Luigi. 1978. Violations of the *Wh*-Island Constraint in Italian and the Subjacency Condition. In Colette Dubisson, David Lightfoot, and Yves-Charles Morin, eds., *Montreal working papers in linguistics 11*, 155–190. McGill University, Montreal.

Rizzi, Luigi. 1982. *Issues in Italian syntax*. Dordrecht: Foris.

Rizzi, Luigi. 1986. Null objects in Italian and the theory of *pro*. *Linguistic Inquiry* 17:501–557.

Rizzi, Luigi. 1990. *Relativized Minimality*. Cambridge, Mass.: MIT Press.

Rizzi, Luigi. 1992. Argument/Adjunct (a)symmetries. In Kimberley Broderick, ed., *NELS 22*, 365–381. Amherst, Mass.: University of Massachusetts, Graduate Linguistic Student Association.

Rizzi, Luigi. 1997. The fine structure of the left periphery. In Liliane Haegeman, ed., *Elements of grammar: Handbook in generative syntax*, 281–337. Dordrecht: Kluwer.

Rizzi, Luigi, ed. 2004. *The cartography of syntactic structures*. Vol. 2, *The structure of CP and IP*. Oxford: Oxford University Press.

Rooth, Mats. 1992. A theory of focus interpretation. *Natural Language Semantics* 1:75–116.

Rooth, Mats. 1996. Focus. In Shalom Lappin, ed., *Handbook of contemporary semantic theory*, 271–297. Oxford: Blackwell.

Runner, Jeffrey T. 1995. Noun phrase licensing and interpretation. Doctoral dissertation, University of Massachusetts, Amherst.

Sabel, Joachim. 2000. Expletives as features. In Roger Billerey and Brook Danielle Lillehaugen, eds., *Proceedings of WCCFL 19*, 411–424. Somerville, Mass.: Cascadilla Press.

Safir, Kenneth J. 1982. Syntactic chains and the definiteness effect. Doctoral dissertation, MIT.

Safir, Kenneth J. 1985. *Syntactic chains*. Cambridge: Cambridge University Press.

Safir, Kenneth J. 1987. What explains the definiteness effect? In Eric J. Reuland and Alice G. B. ter Meulen, eds., *The representation of (in)definiteness*, 71–97. Cambridge, Mass.: MIT Press.

Saito, Mamoru. 1985. Some asymmetries in Japanese and their theoretical implications. Doctoral dissertation, MIT.

Saito, Mamoru. 1989. Scrambling as semantically vacuous A′-movement. In Mark Baltin and Anthony Kroch, eds., *Alternative conceptions of phrase structure*, 182–200. Chicago: University of Chicago Press.

Saito, Mamoru. 1992. Long-distance scrambling in Japanese. *Journal of East Asian Linguistics* 1:69–118.

Saito, Mamoru. 2006. Optional A-scrambling. In Yukinori Takubo, Tomohide Kinuhata, Szymon Grzelak, and Kayo Nagai, eds., *Japanese/Korean linguistics 16*, 44–63. Stanford, Calif.: CSLI Publications.

Sano, Masaki. 1985. LF movement in Japanese. *Descriptive and Applied Linguistics* 18:245–259.

Sansom, G. B. 1928. *A historical grammar of Japanese*. Oxford: Clarendon Press.

Schneider-Zioga, Patricia. 2007. Anti-agreement, anti-locality and minimality: The syntax of dislocated subjects. *Natural Language & Linguistic Theory* 25:403–446.

Sells, Peter. 1995. Korean and Japanese morphology from a lexical perspective. *Linguistic Inquiry* 26:277–325.

Shieber, Stuart M. 1986. *An introduction to unification-based approaches to grammar*. Stanford, Calif.: CSLI Publications.

Shimoyama, Junko. 2001. *Wh*-constructions in Japanese. Doctoral dissertation, University of Massachusetts, Amherst.

Shimoyama, Junko. 2006. Indeterminate phrase quantification in Japanese. *Natural Language Semantics* 14:139–173.

Sigurðsson, Halldór Ármann. 1991. Icelandic case-marked PRO and the licensing of lexical arguments. *Natural Language & Linguistic Theory* 9:327–363.

Sigurðsson, Halldór Ármann. 1996. Icelandic finite verb agreement. *Working Papers in Scandinavian Syntax* 57:1–46.

Sigurðsson, Halldór Ármann. 2003. Meaningful silence, meaningless sounds. Unpublished manuscript, Lund University.

Sigurðsson, Halldór Ármann. 2004. Agree and agreement: Evidence from Germanic. In Werner Abraham, ed., *Focus on Germanic typology*, 61–103. Berlin: Akademie Verlag.

Sigurðsson, Halldór Ármann. 2006. Remarks on features. Unpublished manuscript, Lund University.

Sigurðsson, Halldór Ármann. 2007. On the EPP effects. Unpublished manuscript, Lund University.

Simpson, Andrew, and Zoe Wu. 2001. Agreement, shells, and focus. *Language* 78:287–313.

Sportiche, Dominique. 1988. A theory of floating quantifiers and its corollaries for constituent structure. *Linguistic Inquiry* 19:425–449.

Sportiche, Dominique. 1999. Reconstruction, constituency, and morphology. Paper presented at the 1999 Generative Linguistics in the Old World (GLOW) Colloquium, Berlin.

Sportiche, Dominique. 2006. Reconstruction, binding, and scope. In Martin Everaert and Henk van Riemsdijk, eds., *The Blackwell companion to syntax: Volume IV*, 35–93. Oxford: Blackwell.

Steele, Susan. 1978. Word order variation: A typological study. In Joseph H. Greenberg, Charles A. Ferguson, and Edith A. Moravcsik, eds., *Universals of human language 4: Syntax*, 585–623. Stanford, Calif.: Stanford University Press.

Steriade, Donca. 1987. Locality conditions and feature geometry. In Joyce McDonough and Bernadette Plunkett, eds., *NELS 17*, 595–618. Amherst, Mass.: University of Massachusetts, Graduate Linguistic Student Association.

Stroik, Thomas. 1996. Extraposition and expletive-movement: A minimalist account. *Lingua* 99:237–251.

Sybesma, Rint. 2007. Whether we tense-agree overtly or not. *Linguistic Inquiry* 38:580–587.

Tada, Hiroaki. 1992. Nominative objects in Japanese. *Journal of Japanese Linguistics* 14:91–108.

Tada, Hiroaki. 1993. A/A' partition in derivation. Doctoral dissertation, MIT.

Takahashi, Daiko. 1990. Negative polarity, phrase structure, and the ECP. *English Linguistics* 7:129–146.

Takahashi, Shoichi. 2006. Decompositionality and identity. Doctoral dissertation, MIT.

Takahashi, Shoichi, and Sarah Hulsey. 2009. Wholesale late merger: Beyond the A/Ā distinction. *Linguistic Inquiry* 40.3.

Tanaka, Hidekazu. 1997. Invisible movement in *sika-nai* and the Linear Crossing Constraint. *Journal of East Asian Linguistics* 6:143–178.

Tanaka, Hidekazu. 1999. LF *wh*-islands and the Minimal Scope Principle. *Natural Language & Linguistic Theory* 17:371–402.

Tang, C.-C. Jane. 1985. A study of reflexives in Chinese. Master's thesis, National Taiwan Normal University.

Tang, C.-C. Jane. 1989. Chinese reflexives. *Natural Language & Linguistic Theory* 7:93–121.

Tang, Sze-Wing. 1998. Parametrization of features in syntax. Doctoral dissertation, University of California, Irvine.

Taraldsen, Knut Tarald. 1978. On the NIC, vacuous application, and the *That-t* Filter. Unpublished manuscript, MIT.

Taraldsen, Knut Tarald. 1995. On agreement and nominative objects in Icelandic. In Hubert Haider, Susan Olsen, and Sten Vikner, eds., *Studies in comparative Germanic syntax*, 307–327. Dordrecht: Kluwer.

Taraldsen, Knut Tarald. 1996. Reflexives, pronouns, and subject/V agreement in Icelandic and Faroese. In James Black and Virginia Motapanyane, eds., *Microparametric syntax and dialect variation*, 189–212. Amsterdam: John Benjamins.

Taraldsen, Knut Tarald. 2002. The *que/qui* alternation and the distribution of expletives. In Peter Svenonius, ed., *Subjects, expletives, and the EPP*, 29–42. Oxford: Oxford University Press.

Tenny, Carol. 1994. *Aspectual roles and the syntax-semantics interface*. Dordrecht: Kluwer.

Tenny, Carol. 2006. Evidentiality, experiencers, and the syntax of sentence in Japanese. *Journal of East Asian Linguistics* 15:245–288.

Tomioka, Satoshi. 2007. Pragmatics of LF intervention effects: Japanese and Korean interrogatives. *Journal of Pragmatics* 39:1570–1590.

Tsai, Wei-Tien Dylan. 1994. On nominal islands and LF extraction in Chinese. *Natural Language & Linguistic Theory* 12:121–175.

Tsai, Wei-Tien Dylan. To appear. Tense anchoring in Chinese. *Lingua.*

Ueda, Yukiko. 2006. Ninshoo-seigen-to tougo-kouzou [Person restriction and syntactic structure]. *Scientific Approaches to Language* 5:161–180.

Uriagereka, Juan. 1995. Aspects of the syntax of clitic placement in Western Romance. *Linguistic Inquiry* 26:79–123.

Watanabe, Akira. 1992. Subjacency and S-structure movement of *wh*-in-situ. *Journal of East Asian Linguistics* 1:255–291.

Watanabe, Akira. 2000. Feature copying and binding. *Syntax* 3:159–181.

Watanabe, Akira. 2002. Loss of overt *wh*-movement in Old Japanese. In David W. Lightfoot, ed., *Syntactic effects of morphological change*, 179–195. Oxford: Oxford University Press.

Wexler, Kenneth. 1998. Very early parameter setting and the Unique Checking Constraint. *Lingua* 106:23–79.

Xu, Liejiong. 1986. Free empty category. *Linguistic Inquiry* 17:75–93.

Yang, Dong-Whee. 2004. Scrambling, interpretive complex, and cyclic spell-out. Unpublished manuscript. Seoul National University.

Yoshimura, Noriko. 1989. Parasitic pronouns. Paper presented at the Southern California Conference on Japanese/Korean Linguistics, University of California, Los Angeles.

Yoshimura, Noriko. 1992. Scrambling and anaphora in Japanese. Doctoral dissertation, University of Southern California, Los Angeles.

Yoshimura, Noriko. 1994. 'Ga' no mondai [Issues of *'ga'*]. In *Henyoo-suru gengo bunka kenkyuu*, 13–28. University of Shizuoka, Japan.

Zwart, C. Jan-Wouter. 1993. Dutch syntax: A minimalist approach. Doctoral dissertation, University of Groningen.

Zwart, C. Jan-Wouter. 1997. *A minimalist approach to the syntax of Dutch.* Dordrecht: Kluwer.

Author Index

Alexiadou, Artemis, 2, 28, 36, 43–44, 48, 51, 78, 97, 130

Anagnostopoulou, Elena, 2, 28, 36, 43–44, 48, 51, 78, 97, 130

Anderson, Stephen, 7

Archangeli, Diana, 56

Arikawa, Koji, 65, 68–69

Bahloul, Maher, 4

Baker, C. L., 125, 126

Baker, Mark, 19, 20–22, 45, 94–100

Battistella, Edwin, 50

Beck, Sigrid, 127, 129, 132–134, 135, 138, 139

Belletti, Adriana, 81

Benmamoun, Elabbas, 4

Bhatt, Rajesh, 54, 112

Blight, Robert C., 39

Bobaljik, Jonathan David, 32, 54

Boeckx, Cedric, 3, 16, 38, 45

Boškovi, Željko, 2–3, 5, 38, 40–41

Bowers, John, 39

Brandi, Luciana, 3

Bresnan, Joan, 8

Brody, Michael, 13, 37, 63, 66, 71, 84

Burzio, Luigi, 39

Cable, Seth, 131

Caponigro, Ivano, 39

Carstens, Vicki, 16, 21, 55, 95, 96, 102–103, 105

Chang, Lisa, 132, 133–134

Cheng, Lisa L.-S., 130, 135

Chiercia, Gennaro, 28, 52

Choe, Hyon Sook, 38

Chomsky, Noam, ix–x, 1–2, 3, 4, 5, 7, 9, 10, 11, 16–17, 19–20, 22, 28, 32, 33, 34–36, 37, 38, 43, 52, 56, 59, 65, 78, 110–111, 114, 115–116

Cinque, Guglielmo, 11

Cole, Peter, 50

Cordin, Patricia, 3

Diesing, Molly, 40

Emonds, Joseph, 5

Engdahl, Elisabet, 42

Epstein, Samuel David, 3, 38

Fassi Fehri, Abdelkader, 4

Fox, Danny, x, 31, 65, 110–111, 112, 113

Freidin, Robert, 111

Fukui, Naoki, 1, 59

Gazdar, Gerald, 7

Givón, Talmy, 18

Grewendorf, Günther, 12

Haegeman, Liliane, 16, 55, 57

Hagstrom, Paul, 125, 127, 129, 130, 131, 132, 135, 136, 141

Haig, John H., 68

Halle, Morris, 32

Hamblin, Charles Leonard, 126, 129

Harbert, Wayne, 4

Hasegawa, Nobuko, 15, 62, 63–64, 67, 78, 137

Subject Index

Greek letters are alphabetized according to the English spelling of their names; for example, φ-probe is alphabetized as Phi probe would be, after Phases but before Polysynthesis parameter.

A-/Ā-movement distinction, 37, 60, 109–122
  binding and, 60, 66–67, 69, 109–110
  copy theory of movement and, 110–111
  inheritance of features and, 19–20
  late Merge and, 111–114, 117
  "mixed" positions, 119–120
  phases and, 115–122
  reconstruction and, 65–66, 82, 110, 111, 113, 119–121
Activation, 22
  by Case, 22–23, 27
  by topic/focus, 94, 128–129
  and valuation of features, 22
Agree, 9, 23, 31–32
  uninterpretable features, 7, 31–32
  valuation and, 32
Agreement, purpose of. *See* Purpose of agreement
Agreement, syntactic or morphological, 32
Agreement asymmetry, 3–4
Agreement head, T vs. C, 16
Agreement languages, 10, 11
Agreementless languages, xi, 1, 11
  Japanese, 11
  and the nominal parameter, 27–28
  Strong Uniformity and, 23–26

Agreement–topic/focus parameter, 1, 15–19, 71
  historical evidence, 18
  and inheritance of features, 19, 71
αP, 17, 20–22, 63, 69–71
  in Finnish (αP/TopP), 70, 105–107, 119–120
  in Japanese, 80–83
  in Kikuyu, 70
  in Kilega, 103
  in Kinande, 95–102
  in Romance, 22, 70
Alternatives, semantics of, 129
A-movement, 59–60, 62, 66
  not Case-driven, 2–5, 11, 62, 72–73, 114–115, 117
Ā-movement, 15, 19–20, 48, 49, 61. *See also Wh*-movement
Antiagreement, 23
A-positions, 59, 60
  in Japanese, 69, 73, 82
  Spec,αP, 69–70, 82
  Spec,TP, 59, 73
Arabic, agreement asymmetry in, 4
Arabic, Bani-Hassan, pro-drop in, 44–46
Arbitrariness, of grammatical gender, 6
Argument/adjunct distinction, 112
Argument structure, 10